Node.js for Modern Web Development
Create Scalable Applications

A Comprehensive Guide to Building Server-Side Apps with Node.js

MIGUEL FARMER

RAFAEL SANDERS

Table of Content

TABLE OF CONTENTS

5

INTRODUCTION

Node.js for Modern Web Development: Create Scalable Applications

In today's fast-paced world of web development, building **scalable**, **efficient**, and **maintainable** applications is more crucial than ever. As users demand faster, more responsive websites and applications, the technologies behind these platforms must evolve to meet these challenges. Enter **Node.js**—a powerful, event-driven, non-blocking I/O runtime environment for JavaScript, designed to build fast and scalable network applications.

This book, **"Node.js for Modern Web Development: Create Scalable Applications"**, is aimed at developers of all experience levels who are looking to harness the power of Node.js to build dynamic, high-performance web applications. Whether you are just getting started with Node.js or you're already familiar with its capabilities and want to dive deeper into advanced concepts, this comprehensive guide is designed to take you on a structured learning journey through the world of Node.js and modern web development.

Why Node.js?

Node.js is revolutionizing web development. Traditionally, server-side development involved languages like Java, Python, or PHP. However, Node.js has emerged as a powerful contender in the world of backend development, offering numerous benefits:

- **Non-blocking, Asynchronous I/O**: Node.js is built around an event-driven architecture, making it highly efficient and suitable for building applications that require high concurrency, such as real-time chat applications, gaming platforms, and social media sites.
- **JavaScript on Both Sides**: Node.js enables developers to use JavaScript for both client-side and server-side development, simplifying the development process by enabling the same language across the full stack.
- **Scalability**: Thanks to its **single-threaded** event loop, Node.js is highly capable of handling thousands of concurrent requests, making it ideal for building scalable and distributed systems.
- **Active Ecosystem**: Node.js boasts a thriving ecosystem with a rich set of libraries and frameworks like **Express, Socket.io, GraphQL**, and **Apollo**, making it a one-stop-shop for building everything from simple APIs to complex enterprise-level applications.

In this book, we explore these benefits in-depth while guiding you through real-world applications, helping you implement **modern** and **scalable** solutions using Node.js.

8

What's Inside This Book?

This book is structured to cater to both **beginners** and **experts**, with concepts and examples that progress from basic to advanced levels. It focuses on the full web development lifecycle, from setting up your Node.js environment to deploying production-ready applications. Here's a closer look at what you can expect:

- **Chapter 1: Introduction to Node.js** – A gentle introduction to Node.js and its unique architecture, explaining why Node.js is a great choice for modern web development and how it compares to traditional web servers.

- **Chapter 2: Understanding JavaScript Fundamentals for Node.js** – A deep dive into JavaScript essentials, including ES6+ features like **async/await, Promises**, and **arrow functions**, which are crucial when working with Node.js.

- **Chapter 3: Installing and Setting Up Node.js** – Practical guidance on getting your development environment ready, covering installation on different operating systems, and creating your first Node.js script.

- **Chapter 4: Core Modules in Node.js** – A look at the essential Node.js modules such as **HTTP, File System (fs)**, and **Events**, and how they form the backbone of your server-side logic.

- **Chapter 5: Asynchronous Programming in Node.js** – Learn the fundamentals of **non-blocking I/O**, the **event loop**, and how to handle concurrent requests, which is at the heart of Node.js's performance.

- **Chapter 6: Working with npm** – A comprehensive guide on using **Node Package Manager (npm)** to manage dependencies, install third-party libraries, and even create your own packages.

- **Chapter 7 to Chapter 12: Building RESTful APIs with Express** – This section covers how to use **Express**, the most popular web framework for Node.js, to create REST APIs. We'll discuss routing, middleware, and database integration, as well as **authentication** and **authorization**.

- **Chapter 13: Real-Time Communication with WebSockets** – Discover how to implement real-time communication in your apps using **Socket.io**, ideal for building chat applications, live notifications, and gaming platforms.

- **Chapter 14 to Chapter 16: Testing, Debugging, and Optimizing Node.js Applications** – A crucial section where we discuss techniques to ensure your application is both bug-free and optimized. We will cover testing with **Mocha** and **Jest**, debugging Node.js applications, and optimizing them for performance.

- **Chapter 17 to Chapter 22: Advanced Node.js Patterns and Full-Stack Development** – From **microservices**

architecture to **GraphQL APIs,** this section will show you how to scale your applications and integrate with modern frontend frameworks like **React** and **Vue.js.**

- **Chapter 23: Scaling Node.js Applications** – Learn how to handle massive traffic by scaling Node.js with clustering, load balancing, and using **Redis** for session management.

- **Chapter 24: Future of Node.js and Modern Web Development** – A look into the future of Node.js, with insights on the latest trends in **serverless architecture, edge computing,** and how Node.js will continue to evolve.

Real-World Examples

Throughout the book, we will build **real-world applications** to give you hands-on experience with Node.js. Each chapter features practical, **step-by-step examples**:

- A **blogging platform** where we'll create a REST API and a GraphQL API.
- A **real-time chat application** with **WebSockets.**
- A **scalable e-commerce platform** with **microservices** and **Redis.**

These examples will not only teach you Node.js but also guide you in applying best practices and patterns for creating robust, **production-ready applications**.

Who Is This Book For?

This book is for anyone who wants to become proficient in **Node.js** and **modern web development**. Whether you're:

- A **beginner** eager to learn Node.js and server-side JavaScript, or
- An **experienced developer** looking to master advanced topics like **microservices**, **GraphQL**, and **scaling**, this book will help you advance your skills and understand how to apply Node.js in real-world scenarios.

Why Should You Read This Book?

1. **Practical Approach**: The book is filled with practical examples that show you how to use Node.js to build real-world applications. It's not just theory—you'll learn how to write code, solve problems, and use industry-standard tools.
2. **Scalable Development**: You will learn how to scale your Node.js applications using best practices for **clustering**, **load balancing**, and **caching**, helping you build applications that can handle millions of users.

3. **Comprehensive Coverage**: From setting up the environment to deploying your applications, this book covers every aspect of Node.js and web development.

4. **Modern Tools and Frameworks**: The book doesn't just cover **Node.js**—we dive into other popular tools and frameworks like **Express, GraphQL, Redis**, and **WebSockets** to help you stay up-to-date with modern web development trends.

Final Thoughts

The world of web development is continuously evolving, and **Node.js** is at the forefront of this transformation. Its ability to handle real-time data, scale efficiently, and work seamlessly with JavaScript on both the frontend and backend makes it one of the most popular choices for modern applications. By the end of this book, you will have the skills and knowledge to build **scalable, efficient**, and **robust** web applications using **Node.js**.

Now, let's begin this exciting journey into the world of **Node.js** and modern web development

CHAPTER 1

INTRODUCTION TO NODE.JS

Overview of Node.js

Node.js is a powerful, open-source JavaScript runtime built on Google Chrome's V8 JavaScript engine. It allows developers to write server-side applications in JavaScript, enabling them to create scalable, high-performance applications that can handle multiple simultaneous connections with high throughput.

Historically, JavaScript was primarily a client-side language used for manipulating the DOM and managing browser events. With the introduction of Node.js in 2009, JavaScript could be executed on the server, allowing for the creation of full-stack JavaScript applications.

Node.js is event-driven, non-blocking, and asynchronous by design, making it particularly suitable for real-time applications, APIs, and other high-performance, data-intensive use cases. Its non-blocking I/O model allows the server to handle requests without waiting for previous ones to complete, maximizing efficiency.

14

What Makes Node.js Special for Web Development?

Several features set Node.js apart from traditional server-side programming environments:

1. **Non-blocking, Asynchronous I/O**: Node.js operates in an asynchronous manner, meaning it doesn't wait for a task (like reading from a file or querying a database) to finish before moving on to the next one. This results in high efficiency, especially for applications that handle many I/O-bound operations, such as web servers or APIs.

2. **Single-Threaded Event Loop**: Despite being single-threaded, Node.js can handle many concurrent connections thanks to its event-driven model. The event loop manages tasks asynchronously, preventing the need for creating multiple threads for handling each request, which can be resource-intensive in traditional server environments.

3. **JavaScript Everywhere**: Node.js allows developers to use JavaScript both on the client side and the server side. This unification streamlines the development process and improves productivity by allowing developers to write in a single language across the entire application stack.

4. **Built-in Modules**: Node.js comes with a variety of built-in modules like `http`, `fs`, and `path` that simplify many common tasks such as creating HTTP servers, working

with the file system, and managing URLs, without the need for third-party libraries.

5. **Scalability**: Node.js's event-driven architecture and non-blocking nature make it an excellent choice for building scalable applications that can handle a high volume of requests with low resource consumption. Whether it's horizontal scaling (adding more servers) or vertical scaling (optimizing individual servers), Node.js supports both approaches seamlessly.

Real-World Applications of Node.js

Node.js has gained immense popularity in web development, and many high-profile companies and applications use it to handle a variety of use cases:

1. **Real-Time Applications**: Node.js is perfect for real-time applications such as chat applications, online gaming, and collaborative tools. With libraries like Socket.IO, developers can quickly build systems that support instant communication.

   o **Example**: Slack uses Node.js for real-time messaging and notifications.

2. **Web APIs**: Node.js is ideal for building RESTful APIs due to its fast processing and ability to handle multiple requests concurrently. This makes it popular for creating backend services for mobile apps and websites.

- o **Example**: PayPal uses Node.js to handle its payment APIs, providing a more responsive experience with fewer servers.

3. **Microservices**: The lightweight nature of Node.js makes it a good fit for microservice architectures, where small, independently deployable services communicate with each other to form a complete application.

   - o **Example**: Uber transitioned from monolithic architectures to microservices using Node.js to improve scalability and service reliability.

4. **Streaming Applications**: Node.js is excellent for applications that need to handle a continuous stream of data, such as video streaming, real-time analytics, and IoT applications.

   - o **Example**: Netflix uses Node.js to handle millions of requests and stream video content to its users worldwide.

5. **Command-Line Tools**: Node.js is also used to build powerful command-line tools (CLI) that automate tasks like file management, web scraping, or system monitoring.

   - o **Example**: npm, the package manager used by Node.js, is itself built with Node.js and provides developers with a command-line interface to install and manage dependencies.

Node.js vs. Traditional Web Servers

To better understand the advantages of Node.js, let's compare it with traditional web servers like Apache and Nginx.

1. **Concurrency and Performance**:
   - **Node.js**: Handles multiple concurrent connections in a non-blocking, asynchronous manner, which makes it highly efficient in handling I/O-bound operations.
   - **Traditional Servers**: Apache, for instance, uses a thread-per-request model, meaning a new thread is created for each request. This can be resource-intensive and less scalable for handling many concurrent connections.

2. **Single vs. Multi-Threaded**:
   - **Node.js**: Works on a single-threaded event loop, which allows it to handle many connections without the overhead of managing multiple threads.
   - **Traditional Servers**: Servers like Apache use a multi-threaded or multi-process approach, which can lead to higher memory consumption and slower performance as the number of concurrent requests increases.

3. **Speed**:

- o **Node.js**: Its non-blocking, event-driven architecture allows it to handle requests much faster, especially for I/O-heavy applications like web APIs or real-time applications.
- o **Traditional Servers**: While Apache and Nginx are fast for static content, they struggle with the same level of performance when handling many concurrent connections or dynamic content.

4. **Ease of Development**:

- o **Node.js**: As a JavaScript runtime, Node.js allows developers to write both server-side and client-side code in the same language, improving developer productivity and reducing context switching.
- o **Traditional Servers**: Typically require knowledge of different languages for frontend (HTML, CSS, JavaScript) and backend (PHP, Ruby, Python, etc.), which may lead to a steeper learning curve and more complex development.

Setting Up Your Development Environment

Setting up a Node.js development environment is straightforward and involves the following steps:

1. **Install Node.js and npm**:

- o **Windows**: Download the installer from Node.js official site.
- o **Mac/Linux**: You can use a package manager like `brew` (for Mac) or `apt` (for Linux) to install Node.js. Alternatively, you can download it from the official site.

2. **Verify Installation**: Open your terminal or command prompt and type the following to check that Node.js and npm are installed correctly:

```bash
node -v  # Check Node.js version
npm -v   # Check npm version
```

3. **Create Your First Node.js Application**:
   - o Open your text editor and create a file called `app.js`.
   - o Add the following basic code to create a simple HTTP server:

```javascript
const http = require('http');

const            server             =
http.createServer((req, res) => {
  res.statusCode = 200;
```

20

```
    res.setHeader('Content-Type',
'text/plain');
    res.end('Hello, World!\n');
});

server.listen(3000, () => {
    console.log('Server   running   at
http://localhost:3000/');
});
```

4. **Run Your Application**: In the terminal, navigate to the directory where your app.js file is located and run the following command:

```bash
```

```
node app.js
```

Your server will start running at http://localhost:3000/. Open it in a browser, and you should see the message "Hello, World!" displayed.

5. **Install Dependencies** (Optional): If your application requires external libraries, you can install them via npm. For example, to install Express.js:

```bash
```

```
npm install express
```

21

Conclusion

This chapter introduced you to the basics of Node.js, highlighting its advantages over traditional web servers, its real-world applications, and how to set up a development environment. Understanding these core concepts is the first step in mastering Node.js and building modern web applications with it. In the next chapter, we will dive deeper into JavaScript fundamentals, which will provide the foundation for writing effective Node.js applications.

Let me know if you'd like to add more specifics or examples to any of these sections!

CHAPTER 2

UNDERSTANDING THE BASICS OF JAVASCRIPT

JavaScript Fundamentals for Node.js

Before diving into Node.js, it's crucial to have a solid understanding of JavaScript fundamentals, as Node.js is built entirely on JavaScript. Here are some key JavaScript concepts that will help you as you work with Node.js:

1. **Variables and Data Types**: JavaScript has dynamic typing, meaning variables can hold any data type and can change types during execution. Common data types include:

   o **String**: Text data, e.g., `"Hello, World!"`

   o **Number**: Integer or floating-point numbers, e.g., `42, 3.14`

   o **Boolean**: Represents `true` or `false`

   o **Object**: Key-value pairs, e.g., `{ name: 'John', age: 30 }`

   o **Array**: An ordered list, e.g., `[1, 2, 3]`

   o **Null**: Represents the intentional absence of any object value.

o   **Undefined**: Represents a variable that has been declared but has not been assigned a value.

2. **Functions**: Functions are reusable blocks of code. In JavaScript, functions can be declared in several ways:

```javascript
function sayHello() {
    console.log("Hello, World!");
}
```

3. **Control Flow**: JavaScript supports traditional control flow structures like if, else, switch, for, while, and do...while. These are essential for making decisions and iterating over data.

```javascript
if (x > 10) {
    console.log("x is greater than 10");
} else {
    console.log("x is less than or equal to
10");
}
```

4. **Objects and Arrays**: Objects store collections of key-value pairs, while arrays store ordered lists of values.

```javascript
```

```
let person = { name: "Alice", age: 30 };
let numbers = [1, 2, 3, 4];
```

5. **Scope and Closures**:
   o **Scope** determines the visibility of variables. Variables can be **global** or **local** to a function or block.
   o **Closures** occur when a function "remembers" the environment in which it was created, even after the outer function has finished execution.

```
javascript
```

```javascript
function outer() {
    let outerVar = 'I am outside!';
    return function inner() {
        console.log(outerVar);  // Closure
accessing outer variable
    };
}
let closureExample = outer();
closureExample();  // Outputs:  'I  am
outside!'
```

ES6+ Features (Arrow Functions, Promises, Async/Await)

ES6 (ECMAScript 2015) introduced several new features that simplify JavaScript and make it more powerful, especially when working with Node.js.

1. **Arrow Functions**: Arrow functions provide a concise syntax for writing functions. They also retain the value of `this` from the surrounding lexical context, which is useful when dealing with asynchronous code.

   javascript

   ```
   // Traditional Function
   const add = function(a, b) {
       return a + b;
   };

   // Arrow Function
   const addArrow = (a, b) => a + b;
   ```

2. **Promises**: Promises allow you to handle asynchronous operations more effectively by providing a cleaner syntax and better error handling. They represent a value that may be available now, or in the future, or never.

   javascript

```
const fetchData = new Promise((resolve,
reject) => {
    let               data               =
fetch('http://example.com');
    if (data) {
        resolve(data);
    } else {
        reject('Data fetch failed');
    }
});

fetchData
    .then(response => console.log('Data
fetched:', response))
    .catch(error                      =>
console.error('Error:', error));
```

3. **Async/Await**: `async` and `await` are built on top of Promises and provide an even simpler way to work with asynchronous code. `async` makes a function return a promise, and `await` pauses the execution of the function until the promise resolves.

```
javascript

async function fetchDataAsync() {
    try {
        let     response     =     await
fetch('http://example.com');
```

```
        let data = await response.json();
        console.log(data);
    } catch (error) {
        console.error('Error:', error);
    }
}
```

This approach leads to more readable and maintainable code, especially when working with multiple asynchronous tasks.

The Event Loop and Asynchronous Programming

Node.js's non-blocking nature makes it especially suited for high-concurrency applications. The event loop plays a critical role in how Node.js handles asynchronous code.

1. **What is the Event Loop?** The event loop is a mechanism that allows Node.js to execute non-blocking I/O operations like reading from files, querying a database, or making HTTP requests. It works by pushing tasks (events) into a queue and executing them one by one, without blocking other operations.

2. **Blocking vs. Non-blocking Code**:
    o **Blocking**: In blocking code, the program waits for a task to finish before moving on to the next

28

one. This can lead to poor performance if multiple tasks need to wait for one another to complete.

- o **Non-blocking**: Non-blocking code in Node.js uses the event loop to handle multiple tasks at once, without waiting for any task to finish before starting the next. This ensures the program remains responsive, even under heavy load.

3. **How the Event Loop Works**:

- o **Phase 1**: The event loop starts by executing the initial code (synchronous code).
- o **Phase 2**: It processes the event queue, executing tasks that are added asynchronously.
- o **Phase 3**: Callbacks and Promises that resolve asynchronously are then executed.

A simple example of asynchronous code would be using setTimeout to simulate a delayed operation:

```javascript
console.log('Start');

setTimeout(() => {
    console.log('This    runs    after    2
seconds');
}, 2000);

console.log('End');
```

```
pgsql
```

```
Start
This runs after 2 seconds
```

In this example, `setTimeout` doesn't block the execution of `console.log('End')`. The message `'This runs after 2 seconds'` is printed after the event loop has finished executing the rest of the code.

4. **Callback Queue and Call Stack**: The event loop works in conjunction with the **call stack** and **callback queue**. The call stack holds the synchronous code, and the callback queue holds tasks that are waiting to be executed asynchronously. The event loop picks up tasks from the callback queue once the call stack is clear.

How JavaScript Works in the Browser vs. Node.js

Although JavaScript is used in both the browser and in Node.js, the environments are different in terms of available features and APIs.

1. **JavaScript in the Browser**:

- o **DOM Manipulation**: In the browser, JavaScript interacts with the DOM (Document Object Model), allowing you to modify the content and structure of a webpage dynamically.

- o **Browser APIs**: JavaScript in the browser has access to various browser-specific APIs such as `window`, `document`, and `localStorage` for handling user interface, user input, and local data storage.

- o **Event Handling**: The browser is built around user interactions (clicks, keystrokes, etc.), and JavaScript is used to handle these events.

2. **JavaScript in Node.js**:

- o **Server-Side**: In Node.js, JavaScript is used to build server-side applications, handling HTTP requests, interacting with databases, reading/writing files, and more.

- o **No DOM**: Since Node.js is not running in a browser, it does not have access to the DOM. Instead, it provides other APIs for handling HTTP, file systems, networking, etc.

- o **Modules**: In Node.js, JavaScript uses **modules** to encapsulate functionality, and you can use built-in modules like `fs` (file system), `http` (HTTP server), and `path` (path manipulation).

3. **Global Objects**:

o **In the Browser**: JavaScript has access to `window` as the global object.

o **In Node.js**: The global object is `global`, and you also have access to `process`, which provides information about the current Node.js process (e.g., environment variables, command-line arguments).

Conclusion

In this chapter, we covered essential JavaScript fundamentals that will lay the groundwork for understanding how Node.js works. From the basics of data types and functions to the powerful ES6 features like arrow functions, promises, and async/await, you should now have a clear grasp of the core tools at your disposal. We also explored how asynchronous programming, the event loop, and JavaScript in the browser vs. Node.js differ. Understanding these concepts will enable you to build more efficient and scalable Node.js applications as you progress through this book.

Next, we'll dive deeper into Node.js's built-in modules and how to start building your first server-side application!

Feel free to let me know if you'd like additional examples or clarification on any part of this chapter!

CHAPTER 3

INSTALLING AND SETTING UP NODE.JS

How to Install Node.js on Different Operating Systems

Before you can start building with Node.js, you'll need to install it on your machine. The installation process varies slightly depending on the operating system you're using. Below are the steps for installing Node.js on **Windows**, **MacOS**, and **Linux**.

Windows Installation

1. **Download** **Node.js**:
   Visit the official Node.js website and download the installer suitable for Windows (either the **LTS** or **Current** version).

2. **Run** **the** **Installer**:
   Once the installer is downloaded, double-click the `.msi` file to begin the installation process. Follow the on-screen instructions to install Node.js and npm (Node Package Manager). Make sure to leave the option to install **npm** checked, as it's required for managing Node.js packages.

3. **Verify the Installation**: After the installation, open **Command Prompt** and type the following commands to verify the installation:

```bash
```

```
node -v    # To check the version of Node.js
npm -v     # To check the version of npm
```

You should see the version numbers for both `node` and `npm` printed in the terminal. If this appears, Node.js and npm are installed correctly.

MacOS Installation

1. **Using Homebrew (Recommended)**: If you have **Homebrew** installed, you can use it to install Node.js easily. Open your terminal and run the following commands:

```bash
```

```
brew install node
```

If you don't have Homebrew installed, you can install it by running:

```bash
```

```
/bin/bash         -c        "$(curl        -fsSL
https://raw.githubusercontent.com/Homebre
w/install/HEAD/install.sh)"
```

2. **Verify the Installation**: Once the installation is complete, check the version of Node.js and npm by typing:

```
bash


node -v
npm -v
```

You should see the installed versions.

3. **Alternative Method (Using the Installer)**:
   o Download the Node.js installer from Node.js official website.
   o Run the installer and follow the instructions, similar to the Windows process.

Linux Installation

1. **Using apt (Debian/Ubuntu-based distributions)**: Open a terminal window and type the following commands:

```
bash


sudo apt update
sudo apt install nodejs npm
```

2. **Verify the Installation**: After installation is complete, verify the Node.js and npm installation:

```bash
node -v
npm -v
```

3. **Alternative Method (Using Node Version Manager - nvm)**: If you want more control over the Node.js versions, you can use **nvm** (Node Version Manager). This allows you to install and switch between different versions of Node.js:

```bash
curl                                    -o-
https://raw.githubusercontent.com/nvm-
sh/nvm/v0.39.0/install.sh | bash
```

After installing nvm, install Node.js with:

```bash
nvm install node   # Install the latest
version of Node.js
```

Using the Node.js REPL (Read-Eval-Print Loop)

The **Node.js REPL** (Read-Eval-Print Loop) is an interactive shell that allows you to execute JavaScript code in real-time. It's a useful tool for testing snippets of JavaScript or experimenting with the language.

Starting the Node.js REPL

To launch the REPL, simply open a terminal or command prompt and type:

```bash
bash
```

```
node
```

You should see the Node.js prompt >, indicating that you're in the REPL environment.

Basic Commands in the REPL

1. **Evaluate Expressions**: You can write any JavaScript expression and the REPL will evaluate it immediately.

   ```bash
   bash
   ```

   ```
   > 2 + 2
   4
   ```

2. **Declare Variables**: You can declare variables just like in JavaScript:

bash

```
> let name = "Node.js"
> name
'Node.js'
```

3. **Call Functions**: You can also define and call functions directly in the REPL:

bash

```
> function greet() { return "Hello, Node!"
}
> greet()
'Hello, Node!'
```

4. **Exit the REPL**: To exit the REPL, type .exit or press Ctrl+C twice.

Understanding npm (Node Package Manager)

npm is the default package manager for Node.js. It allows you to install and manage third-party libraries and dependencies for your Node.js applications.

39

What is npm?

- **npm** connects to a massive online registry (npm registry), where thousands of JavaScript packages (libraries) are available for use. These packages help extend the functionality of your Node.js apps by providing pre-built solutions for common problems (e.g., Express for web servers, Lodash for utility functions, etc.).

Using npm:

1. **Initializing a Project**: To start using npm, you first need to create a `package.json` file, which tracks all your project's dependencies. Run the following command to initialize a new Node.js project:

   bash

   ```
   npm init
   ```

   This will prompt you to answer a few questions about your project (name, version, entry point, etc.). If you want to skip the questions, you can run:

   bash

   ```
   npm init -y
   ```

2. **Installing Dependencies**: To install a package (e.g., Express), you can run:

```bash

npm install express --save
```

The `--save` flag ensures that the package is added to your `package.json` file, so other developers or deployment systems can install the same dependencies.

3. **Viewing Installed Packages**: You can list all installed packages using:

```bash

npm list
```

4. **Installing Global Packages**: Sometimes, you may need to install packages globally, for example, `nodemon` (a tool for automatically restarting your Node.js server). You can do this with:

```bash

npm install -g nodemon
```

5. **Uninstalling a Package**: To remove a package, run:

```
bash
```

```
npm uninstall express
```

6. **Updating Packages**: To update all installed packages to their latest versions, run:

```
bash
```

```
npm update
```

Your First Node.js Script

Once Node.js is installed and you're comfortable with the basics of npm, it's time to write your first Node.js script.

Creating a Simple HTTP Server:

Let's create a simple HTTP server using Node.js's built-in `http` module.

1. **Create   a   File**: Create a file called `app.js` in your project directory.

2. **Write the Code**: In `app.js`, write the following code to create a basic HTTP server:

```
javascript
```

```
const http = require('http');

const server = http.createServer((req,
res) => {
    res.statusCode = 200;  // HTTP status
code
    res.setHeader('Content-Type',
'text/plain');
    res.end('Hello, World!\n');
});

server.listen(3000, () => {
    console.log('Server     running     at
http://localhost:3000/');
});
```

3. **Run the Script**: Open your terminal, navigate to your project folder, and run:

```bash

node app.js
```

You should see the message "Server running at http://localhost:3000/" in your terminal. Open a browser and visit http://localhost:3000/—you should see "Hello, World!" displayed.

Handling Errors in Node.js

Error handling is an essential part of any application. In Node.js, errors can occur in synchronous code, asynchronous code, or during I/O operations. Let's go over how to handle errors properly.

Synchronous Errors:

For synchronous errors, you can use the standard `try...catch` block to catch exceptions:

```javascript
try {
    let result = riskyFunction(); // Function
that might throw an error
} catch (error) {
    console.error('Error occurred:', error);
}
```

Asynchronous Errors:

For asynchronous code, Node.js provides error handling through **callbacks** and **Promises**.

1. **Callbacks**: When dealing with callback-based APIs, always pass an error object as the first parameter. For example:

```javascript
fs.readFile('file.txt', 'utf8', (err,
data) => {
    if (err) {
        console.error('Error    reading
file:', err);
        return;
    }
    console.log('File content:', data);
});
```

2. **Promises**: In asynchronous code that uses Promises, you can handle errors using `.catch()`:

```javascript
fetchDataFromApi()
    .then(data => console.log(data))
    .catch(err => console.error('Error:',
err));
```

3. **Async/Await**: For `async/await`, you can use a `try...catch` block to handle errors in asynchronous functions:

```javascript
async function fetchData() {
    try {
```

45

```
        let     response     =     await
fetch('http://example.com');
        let data = await response.json();
        console.log(data);
    } catch (error) {
        console.error('Error      fetching
data:', error);
    }
}
```

Conclusion

In this chapter, we've covered the process of installing and setting up Node.js on different operating systems, using the Node.js REPL for interactive code execution, and understanding the npm package manager. We also walked through creating a basic HTTP server and how to handle errors effectively in Node.js. With this foundation, you're ready to start building more complex applications and utilizing npm packages to enhance your Node.js projects.

In the next chapter, we'll dive deeper into the core modules in Node.js, helping you understand how to leverage built-in functionality to build powerful web applications.

CHAPTER 4

CORE MODULES IN NODE.JS

Node.js provides several built-in modules that make it easy to build robust and efficient applications. In this chapter, we will dive into some of the core modules that are commonly used in server-side applications. These modules include **File System (fs)**, the **HTTP module** for web servers, **Path, URL, and Query modules**, and the **Event module**. By understanding these modules, you'll be able to handle file operations, create web servers, manage URLs, and handle events with ease.

File System (fs)

The **fs** module provides a set of functions to interact with the file system, allowing you to read from and write to files, create directories, and more.

Basic File Operations with fs

1. **Reading Files**: Node.js provides both synchronous and asynchronous methods for reading files.

   o **Asynchronous File Reading**:

   ```javascript
   ```

```
const fs = require('fs');

fs.readFile('example.txt',    'utf8',
(err, data) => {
    if (err) {
        console.log('Error   reading
file:', err);
        return;
    }
    console.log('File    content:',
data);
});
```

o **Synchronous File Reading**:

```javascript
const fs = require('fs');

try {
    const          data          =
fs.readFileSync('example.txt',
'utf8');
    console.log('File    content:',
data);
} catch (err) {
    console.log('Error        reading
file:', err);
}
```

2. **Writing Files**: You can write data to files using `writeFile` (asynchronous) or `writeFileSync` (synchronous).

- **Asynchronous File Writing**:

```javascript
const fs = require('fs');

const content = 'Hello, Node.js!';
fs.writeFile('output.txt', content, (err) => {
    if (err) {
        console.log('Error writing file:', err);
        return;
    }
    console.log('File written successfully!');
});
```

- **Synchronous File Writing**:

```javascript
const fs = require('fs');

const content = 'Hello, Node.js!';
try {
```

```
        fs.writeFileSync('output.txt',
content);
        console.log('File        written
successfully!');
    } catch (err) {
        console.log('Error        writing
file:', err);
    }
```

3. **Creating Directories**: The `fs` module also allows you to create directories.

```javascript
const fs = require('fs');

fs.mkdir('newFolder', (err) => {
    if (err) {
        console.log('Error        creating
directory:', err);
        return;
    }
    console.log('Directory        created
successfully!');
});
```

HTTP Module for Web Servers

The **http** module in Node.js allows you to create a basic web server that can handle HTTP requests and serve responses. This module is essential for building web applications.

Creating a Simple HTTP Server

1. **Basic HTTP Server**: To create a simple HTTP server using Node.js, you can use the http.createServer() method. This method accepts a callback that will handle incoming requests.

```javascript
const http = require('http');

const server = http.createServer((req, res) => {
    res.statusCode = 200;   // HTTP status code for success
    res.setHeader('Content-Type', 'text/plain');   // Setting the response header
    res.end('Hello, World!');   // Sending the response
});

server.listen(3000, () => {
```

```
console.log('Server      running      at
http://localhost:3000/');
});
```

- o **Explanation**:
  - `req` (request) is an object containing information about the incoming request, such as the URL, headers, and data sent with the request.
  - `res` (response) is an object used to send a response back to the client.
  - The server listens on port `3000` and outputs the message "Hello, World!" when a request is received.

2. **Handling Different Routes**: You can handle different routes and respond accordingly by checking the URL of the incoming request.

```javascript
const http = require('http');

const server = http.createServer((req, res) => {
    if (req.url === '/') {
        res.statusCode = 200;
        res.setHeader('Content-Type',
'text/html');
```

```
        res.end('<h1>Welcome to the Home
Page!</h1>');
    } else if (req.url === '/about') {
        res.statusCode = 200;
        res.setHeader('Content-Type',
'text/html');
        res.end('<h1>About Us</h1>');
    } else {
        res.statusCode = 404;
        res.end('<h1>Page                Not
Found</h1>');
    }
});

server.listen(3000, () => {
    console.log('Server     running     at
http://localhost:3000/');
});
```

Path, URL, and Query Modules

Node.js includes several modules to help with URL handling, path manipulation, and querying.

Path Module

The **path** module provides utilities for working with file and directory paths. It can be used to join, resolve, and manipulate paths.

1. **Joining Paths**:

```javascript
const path = require('path');

const filePath = path.join(__dirname, 'files', 'example.txt');
console.log(filePath);
```

2. **Resolving Absolute Paths**:

```javascript
const path = require('path');

const absolutePath = path.resolve('example.txt');
console.log(absolutePath);
```

3. **Extracting File Extensions**:

```javascript
```

```
const path = require('path');

const ext = path.extname('example.txt');
console.log(ext);   // Outputs: '.txt'
```

URL Module

The **url** module helps with parsing and formatting URLs.

1. **Parsing a URL**:

   javascript

   ```
   const url = require('url');

   const                parsedUrl               =
   url.parse('http://www.example.com/path?na
   me=JohnDoe&id=123');
   console.log(parsedUrl);
   ```

2. **Creating a URL**:

   javascript

   ```
   const url = require('url');

   const formattedUrl = url.format({
       protocol: 'http',
       hostname: 'www.example.com',
       pathname: '/path',
       query: { name: 'JohnDoe', id: '123' }
   ```

55

```
});
```

```
console.log(formattedUrl);
```

Query Module

The **querystring** module provides utilities for parsing and formatting query strings.

1. **Parsing Query Strings**:

   javascript

   ```javascript
   const          querystring          =
   require('querystring');
   ```

   ```javascript
   const          query          =
   querystring.parse('name=JohnDoe&id=123');
   console.log(query);   // Outputs: { name:
   'JohnDoe', id: '123' }
   ```

2. **Stringifying Query Objects**:

   javascript

   ```javascript
   const          querystring          =
   require('querystring');
   ```

   ```javascript
   const          queryString          =
   querystring.stringify({ name: 'JohnDoe',
   id: '123' });
   ```

56

```
console.log(queryString);      // Outputs:
'name=JohnDoe&id=123'
```

Event Module and Event Emitters

The **events** module in Node.js is an essential part of event-driven programming. It allows you to create custom events and handle them using event listeners. The core class here is the **EventEmitter**.

Creating an EventEmitter

1. **Basic EventEmitter**: To create custom events, you first need to create an instance of the `EventEmitter` class and then bind listeners to specific events.

    ```javascript
    const EventEmitter = require('events');
    const emitter = new EventEmitter();

    // Listen for an event
    emitter.on('greet', () => {
        console.log('Hello, World!');
    });

    // Emit the event
    emitter.emit('greet');
    ```

2. **Passing Arguments to Event Listeners**: Event listeners can receive arguments when an event is emitted:

javascript

```javascript
emitter.on('greet', (name) => {
    console.log(`Hello, ${name}!`);
});


emitter.emit('greet',   'Alice');        //
Outputs: 'Hello, Alice!'
```

3. **Event Handling with Multiple Listeners**: You can add multiple listeners to the same event:

javascript

```javascript
emitter.on('greet', () => {
    console.log('First listener');
});


emitter.on('greet', () => {
    console.log('Second listener');
});


emitter.emit('greet');
```

Output:

sql

```
First listener
Second listener
```

4. **Removing Listeners**: You can remove specific event listeners using the `.removeListener()` or `.off()` methods.

```javascript
const greetListener = () =>
console.log('Hello!');
emitter.on('greet', greetListener);
emitter.removeListener('greet',
greetListener);
emitter.emit('greet');   // No output, as
the listener has been removed
```

Real-World Example: Creating a Simple HTTP Server

Let's combine everything we've covered so far into a real-world example of creating a simple HTTP server that serves files and handles events.

```javascript
const http = require('http');
const fs = require('fs');
const path = require('path');
```

```
const EventEmitter = require('events');

const emitter = new EventEmitter();

// Listen for a custom event
emitter.on('fileRequested', (fileName) => {
    console.log(`File requested: ${fileName}`);
});

// Create the server
const server = http.createServer((req, res) => {
    const filePath = path.join(__dirname,
'public', req.url);

    // Emit custom event when a file is requested
    emitter.emit('fileRequested', req.url);

    // Serve the requested file
    fs.readFile(filePath, 'utf8', (err, data) =>
{
        if (err) {
            res.statusCode = 404;
            res.end('File not found');
            return;
        }
        res.statusCode = 200;
        res.setHeader('Content-Type',
'text/html');
        res.end(data);
```

```
    });
});

// Start the server
server.listen(3000, () => {
    console.log('Server          running          at
http://localhost:3000/');
});
```

- **Explanation**: The server listens for HTTP requests and serves files from a `public` directory. It emits a custom event (`fileRequested`) whenever a file is requested, logging the file name to the console.

Conclusion

In this chapter, we've explored some of the most important core modules in Node.js, including **fs** for file handling, **http** for creating web servers, **path**, **url**, and **query** for managing paths and URLs, and the **events** module for event-driven programming. These modules are fundamental for building efficient and scalable applications in Node.js, and mastering them is essential as you continue developing with Node.js.

In the next chapter, we will dive deeper into handling requests and responses with Express.js, building on the knowledge you've gained so far.

CHAPTER 5

THE NODE.JS EVENT LOOP AND NON-BLOCKING I/O

In this chapter, we will explore one of the most significant features of Node.js: its **non-blocking I/O** and **event-driven architecture**. These features enable Node.js to handle multiple concurrent connections efficiently without waiting for each task to complete before moving on to the next one. We'll explain how the event loop works, the difference between blocking and non-blocking code, and how Node.js handles concurrent requests. Finally, we will build a real-world example to demonstrate these concepts in action.

Understanding Blocking vs. Non-Blocking Code

In most programming environments, when a program performs an I/O operation—such as reading a file, querying a database, or making an HTTP request—the program **blocks** execution until the operation completes. This can lead to inefficiency, especially when handling multiple tasks simultaneously.

Blocking Code

Blocking code is synchronous. The program execution halts while waiting for a task (like reading from a file or querying a database) to finish. Only when the task completes does the program proceed with the next operation.

Example of blocking code:

```javascript

const fs = require('fs');

console.log('Start reading file');

// This is blocking code
const data = fs.readFileSync('example.txt', 'utf8');
console.log('File content:', data);

console.log('End of program');
```

In the above example, the program will stop at the `fs.readFileSync()` line until the file has been fully read. This means that any other operation—such as logging 'End of program' or handling other requests—has to wait until the file is fully read, resulting in delays.

Non-Blocking Code

Non-blocking code, on the other hand, allows the program to continue executing while an I/O operation is being processed. In Node.js, non-blocking I/O operations use **asynchronous programming**—tasks are initiated and then moved to the background, allowing other tasks to run while waiting for the response.

Example of non-blocking code:

```javascript
const fs = require('fs');

console.log('Start reading file');

// This is non-blocking code
fs.readFile('example.txt', 'utf8', (err, data) => {
    if (err) throw err;
    console.log('File content:', data);
});

console.log('End of program');
```

In this case, the program doesn't wait for the file to be read. It logs 'End of program' immediately after initiating the read operation, and when the file is finally read, the callback function is triggered to display the file content.

The Event-Driven Architecture

Node.js is designed around an **event-driven architecture**. The core idea is that the application listens for certain events and responds to them when they occur, rather than executing tasks sequentially. This model is particularly useful for handling I/O-bound operations, like reading files, making HTTP requests, or querying a database.

1. **The Event Loop**: At the heart of Node.js's non-blocking architecture is the **event loop**. The event loop is a mechanism that continuously checks for tasks (events) to execute and processes them asynchronously.

2. **Callbacks and Event Emitters**: When Node.js performs an asynchronous operation (like reading a file or querying a database), it places the operation in the **callback queue**. Once the operation is completed, a callback function is triggered to process the result. This process is event-driven because it revolves around emitting and handling events.

How Node.js Handles Concurrent Requests

Node.js is **single-threaded** by design, but it can handle multiple concurrent requests efficiently. This is because it doesn't create a new thread for each request. Instead, it uses an **event-driven, non-blocking I/O** model. Here's how it works:

1. **Single-Threaded Execution**: Node.js runs on a single thread (the main thread). Instead of waiting for one task to complete before starting the next, it delegates I/O operations to the system kernel (which is optimized for handling I/O tasks) and continues processing other tasks.

2. **Event Loop**: The event loop is responsible for processing tasks (events). While the event loop runs, Node.js can handle many requests concurrently by delegating time-consuming operations to the system kernel. This model ensures that Node.js doesn't get bogged down by waiting for I/O operations to complete.

3. **Non-Blocking I/O**: When a request comes in, Node.js immediately returns a response or starts processing. It doesn't block the entire process while waiting for something to complete. Instead, it moves on to other requests while the I/O operations (like reading a file or making a network request) happen in the background.

4. **Concurrency without Threads**: Node.js achieves concurrency by using **callbacks** and **promises** to handle asynchronous tasks. It can initiate multiple I/O operations

67

at the same time and only processes them once they've completed. The event loop efficiently handles the execution order of tasks in the queue.

Real-World Example: Building an Async Web App

Let's create a simple Node.js web app that simulates fetching data from an external source (like a database or an API). This example will help demonstrate how Node.js handles asynchronous requests, improving scalability and performance.

Step 1: Setting Up the Project

First, create a new folder for the project and initialize the Node.js project.

```bash
bash

mkdir async-web-app
cd async-web-app
npm init -y
```

Next, create a file called app.js where we will write our code.

Step 2: Writing the Async Web App

Here's how we can create an asynchronous web app using the **http** module and simulate fetching data from an external source using setTimeout (to mimic the time delay of I/O operations):

javascript

```
const http = require('http');

// Simulating an async operation like database
querying
function fetchData(callback) {
    setTimeout(() => {
        console.log('Fetching data...');
        callback('Data fetched successfully');
    }, 2000); // Simulating 2 seconds delay
}

const server = http.createServer((req, res) => {
    console.log('Received a request');

    // Handling the request asynchronously
    fetchData((data) => {
        res.statusCode = 200;
        res.setHeader('Content-Type',
'text/plain');
        res.end(data); // Sending the fetched
data as the response
```

```
    });
});

server.listen(3000, () => {
    console.log('Server          running          at
http://localhost:3000/');
});
```

Step 3: Running the App

1. In the terminal, navigate to your project folder and run the app:

```
bash
```

```
node app.js
```

2. Open your browser and visit http://localhost:3000/. You'll see "Data fetched successfully" after a 2-second delay.

Explanation:

- When a request comes in, the server does not block the entire process while waiting for the simulated fetchData function to complete. Instead, it immediately moves on to handle other requests.

- The setTimeout function simulates an asynchronous operation (e.g., a database query or API call), and once the operation completes, it calls the callback function to send the result back to the client.

- The server remains responsive even while waiting for the data to be fetched, showcasing how Node.js handles multiple requests concurrently without blocking.

Conclusion

In this chapter, we've explored how Node.js achieves non-blocking I/O through its **event-driven architecture**. We discussed the differences between blocking and non-blocking code and how the **event loop** allows Node.js to handle multiple requests efficiently on a single thread. Finally, we built a real-world example of an asynchronous web app to demonstrate how Node.js can handle tasks concurrently, making it well-suited for high-performance applications.

In the next chapter, we'll dive into **Express.js**, a minimal web framework built on top of Node.js, which will simplify many of the tasks we covered here and allow us to build robust web applications even more easily.

CHAPTER 6

WORKING WITH NPM (NODE PACKAGE MANAGER)

The **Node Package Manager (npm)** is an essential tool for any Node.js developer. It allows you to manage libraries and dependencies, automate tasks, and share your own code with the community. In this chapter, we will cover how to manage project dependencies, use the `package.json` file for project management, understand the difference between global and local npm packages, and even create your first npm package. We'll finish with a real-world example of how to use npm packages like **Express.js** to build a web application.

Managing Dependencies

Dependencies are libraries or modules that your project needs in order to function properly. npm makes it easy to manage these dependencies by allowing you to install, update, and uninstall packages.

Installing Dependencies:

To install a package and add it to your project's dependencies, use the following command:

```bash
```

```bash
npm install <package-name>
```

For example, to install **Express.js** (a web framework for Node.js):

```bash
```

```bash
npm install express
```

This command installs the **Express** package and adds it to your node_modules directory (where npm stores installed packages).

Saving Dependencies to package.json:

By default, when you install a package using npm install, it's added to the node_modules folder but **not** recorded in the package.json file unless you use the --save flag (this is done automatically for most recent versions of npm).

To explicitly save a package as a dependency, run:

```bash
```

```
npm install express --save
```

You can also install **devDependencies** (dependencies needed for development, like testing libraries):

```
bash
```

```
npm install jest --save-dev
```

Using package.json for Project Management

The **package.json** file is the heart of your Node.js project. It contains metadata about the project, such as its name, version, author, and the dependencies it relies on. It also helps manage npm scripts and configuration for your project.

Creating package.json:

You can create a package.json file manually, but it's more common to use the following command to initialize it:

```
bash
```

```
npm init
```

This will prompt you for various details about your project (name, version, description, entry point, etc.), and generate the package.json file.

To skip the prompts and generate a `package.json` with default values, use:

```bash
npm init -y
```

Sample package.json:

Here's a simple example of a `package.json` file:

```json
{
  "name": "my-app",
  "version": "1.0.0",
  "description": "A simple Node.js app",
  "main": "app.js",
  "scripts": {
    "start": "node app.js",
    "test": "jest"
  },
  "dependencies": {
    "express": "^4.17.1"
  },
  "devDependencies": {
    "jest": "^26.6.3"
  },
  "author": "Your Name",
  "license": "MIT"
```

```
}
```

In this example:

- **dependencies**: Packages required for the app to run in production (like **Express**).
- **devDependencies**: Packages needed for development (like **Jest** for testing).
- **scripts**: Custom commands for managing the project (e.g., `npm start` to run your app or `npm test` to run tests).

Global vs Local npm Packages

npm allows you to install packages either **globally** or **locally**.

Local Packages:

A local npm package is installed within your project directory, typically under the `node_modules` folder. These packages are specific to your project and will be referenced in your `package.json` file.

When you run:

```bash
bash
```

```
npm install <package-name>
```

The package is installed locally.

Global Packages:

Global npm packages are installed globally on your system and are available for use in any project. These are typically tools that you use across multiple projects (e.g., build tools, linters, or task runners).

To install a package globally, use the -g flag:

```
bash
```

```
npm install -g <package-name>
```

For example:

```
bash
```

```
npm install -g nodemon
```

Now, nodemon will be available globally from the command line, and you can use it to restart your server automatically when code changes.

Listing Installed Global Packages:

To list the globally installed packages, use:

```bash
bash
```

```
npm list -g --depth=0
```

Uninstalling Global Packages:

To uninstall a global package:

```bash
bash
```

```
npm uninstall -g <package-name>
```

Creating Your First npm Package

Creating your own npm package is a great way to share reusable code with the community or with your team. Here's how you can create and publish a simple npm package.

Step 1: Create the Package:

Let's say you have a simple function in a file called `index.js` that you want to turn into a reusable npm package.

Example `index.js`:

```javascript
javascript
```

```javascript
function greet(name) {
    return `Hello, ${name}!`;
```

```
}
```

```
module.exports = greet;
```

Step 2: Initialize the Package:

In the same folder as your `index.js` file, initialize a new npm package:

```bash
```

```
npm init
```

This will prompt you to fill in details for your package (e.g., name, version, description). Make sure to provide a unique name for your package.

Step 3: Publish the Package:

Once your `package.json` is ready, you can publish your package to the npm registry.

First, make sure you have an npm account. If you don't, you can create one by running:

```bash
```

```
npm adduser
```

Then, publish your package:

```bash
bash
```

```bash
npm publish
```

Your package is now publicly available for other developers to install and use!

Step 4: Installing Your Package:

To install your package in another project, run:

```bash
bash
```

```bash
npm install <your-package-name>
```

Real-World Example: Using Express.js to Build a Web App

Now that we've covered the basics of npm, let's create a simple web application using **Express.js**, which is one of the most popular npm packages for building web applications in Node.js.

Step 1: Initialize the Project:

Start by creating a new project folder and initializing it:

```bash
bash
```

```bash
mkdir express-app
cd express-app
```

```
npm init -y
```

Step 2: Install Express.js:

Install Express.js using npm:

```bash
npm install express --save
```

Step 3: Create the Web App:

Create a file called `app.js` and add the following code to set up a basic web server:

```javascript
const express = require('express');
const app = express();
const port = 3000;

// Middleware to serve static files
app.use(express.static('public'));

// Home route
app.get('/', (req, res) => {
    res.send('<h1>Welcome to Express.js!</h1>');
});

// Start the server
app.listen(port, () => {
```

```
console.log(`Server        running        at
http://localhost:${port}/`);
});
```

Step 4: Running the App:

Run your app using the command:

```
bash
```

```
node app.js
```

You should now have a simple web app running on `http://localhost:3000/`. The app will display a welcome message when you visit the homepage.

Step 5: Add a Static File:

Create a folder named `public` and add an `index.html` file with some basic content. The server will automatically serve static files from the `public` directory.

Example `public/index.html`:

```
html
```

```html
<!DOCTYPE html>
<html>
<head>
    <title>My First Express App</title>
```

```
</head>
<body>
    <h1>Hello from the static HTML page!</h1>
</body>
</html>
```

Now, if you visit `http://localhost:3000/`, the server will serve the static `index.html` file.

Conclusion

In this chapter, we've covered how to work with npm, including managing project dependencies, using the `package.json` file, understanding the difference between global and local packages, and creating your own npm package. We also built a real-world web application using **Express.js** to demonstrate how npm packages can be utilized in your Node.js projects.

In the next chapter, we'll dive deeper into handling requests and responses with **Express.js**, including routing, middleware, and building RESTful APIs.

CHAPTER 7

INTRODUCTION TO EXPRESS.JS

Express.js is a popular web framework for **Node.js** that simplifies the process of building robust, scalable, and maintainable web applications and APIs. In this chapter, we'll cover the essentials of **Express.js**, including its features, how to set up a simple server, and how to handle routing and middleware. We'll finish with a real-world example of building a **RESTful API** with Express.js.

What is Express.js?

Express.js is a minimal, flexible, and lightweight framework for building web applications and APIs in **Node.js**. It provides a simple API for creating server-side applications and handling HTTP requests, making it a popular choice for web developers.

Some of the key features of Express.js include:

- **Routing**: Easily manage different HTTP requests (GET, POST, PUT, DELETE) and map them to specific route handlers.

- **Middleware**: Use middleware functions to process requests before they reach the route handler or after the response is sent.
- **Templating**: Render dynamic HTML views using templating engines like **EJS**, **Pug**, or **Handlebars**.
- **Static Files**: Serve static assets like images, CSS, and JavaScript files.
- **Error Handling**: Simplify error handling with centralized management.

Express.js abstracts much of the complexity involved in handling HTTP requests and responses, making it easier to develop applications with **Node.js**.

Setting Up Your First Express Server

Setting up an Express server is straightforward. Let's walk through the steps to create a simple Express server.

Step 1: Install Express.js

First, you need to initialize your project and install Express.js via npm.

1. **Create a project folder** and navigate into it:

    bash

```
mkdir express-server
cd express-server
```

2. **Initialize the project** (this will create a `package.json` file):

```bash
npm init -y
```

3. **Install Express**:

```bash
npm install express --save
```

Step 2: Create the Express Server

Create a file called `app.js` in the project folder. This file will contain the setup for your Express server.

```javascript
const express = require('express');
const app = express();
const port = 3000;

// Basic route
app.get('/', (req, res) => {
    res.send('Hello, Express!');
```

86

```
});
```

```
// Start the server
app.listen(port, () => {
    console.log(`Server    is    running    at
http://localhost:${port}`);
});
```

Step 3: Running the Server

1. **Start the server** by running the following command:

   ```bash
   node app.js
   ```

2. Open your browser and visit `http://localhost:3000/`. You should see the message **"Hello, Express!"** displayed.

Routing Basics in Express

Routing in Express.js is the mechanism that allows you to define how the server should respond to various HTTP requests at different URLs or paths.

Creating Routes

Routes are defined using the **app.get()**, **app.post()**, **app.put()**, and **app.delete()** methods (and others for other HTTP methods).

1. **GET Route**:
   - This route handles HTTP GET requests and is typically used to retrieve data.

   javascript

   ```javascript
   app.get('/home', (req, res) => {
       res.send('Welcome to the Home Page!');
   });
   ```

2. **POST Route**:
   - This route handles HTTP POST requests, typically used to submit data.

   javascript

   ```javascript
   app.post('/submit', (req, res) => {
       res.send('Form                submitted
   successfully!');
   });
   ```

3. **PUT Route**:
   - This route handles HTTP PUT requests, typically used to update existing resources.

```
javascript
```

```javascript
app.put('/update/:id', (req, res) => {
    const id = req.params.id;
    res.send(`Updating resource with ID:
${id}`);
});
```

4. **DELETE Route**:

   o This route handles HTTP DELETE requests, typically used to delete resources.

```
javascript
```

```javascript
app.delete('/delete/:id', (req, res) => {
    const id = req.params.id;
    res.send(`Deleting resource with ID:
${id}`);
});
```

Route Parameters

Express allows you to define **route parameters** within the URL, which can be accessed via req.params. For example:

```
javascript
```

```javascript
app.get('/user/:id', (req, res) => {
    const userId = req.params.id;
    res.send(`User ID is: ${userId}`);
```

```
});
```

When visiting `/user/123`, the server will respond with `User ID is: 123`.

Middleware in Express

Middleware functions are functions that have access to the request (`req`), response (`res`), and the next middleware function in the application's request-response cycle. They can modify the request, the response, or terminate the request-response cycle.

Common Uses of Middleware:

- Logging requests
- Validating user input
- Authenticating requests
- Serving static files

Basic Middleware Example

Let's set up a middleware that logs the HTTP method and URL of each incoming request:

```javascript
app.use((req, res, next) => {
    console.log(`${req.method} ${req.url}`);
```

```
next(); // Passes control to the next
middleware or route handler
});
```

Built-in Middleware:

Express comes with some built-in middleware, such as:

- `express.static()` to serve static files (e.g., images, CSS files).
- `express.json()` to parse incoming JSON data.
- `express.urlencoded()` to parse URL-encoded data.

Example of using built-in middleware to parse JSON data in requests:

javascript

```
app.use(express.json());
```

Real-World Example: A Simple RESTful API with Express

Let's build a simple **RESTful API** that can perform CRUD (Create, Read, Update, Delete) operations on a list of users. For simplicity, we will use an in-memory array to store user data, but in real-world applications, this would typically be a database.

Step 1: Define the API Routes

Create a new file `app.js`:

```
javascript


const express = require('express');
const app = express();
const port = 3000;

app.use(express.json()); // Middleware to parse
JSON request bodies

// In-memory user database
let users = [
    { id: 1, name: 'John Doe' },
    { id: 2, name: 'Jane Smith' }
];

// Get all users (Read)
app.get('/users', (req, res) => {
    res.json(users);
});

// Get user by ID (Read)
app.get('/users/:id', (req, res) => {
    const user = users.find(u => u.id ===
parseInt(req.params.id));
    if (!user) return res.status(404).send('User
not found');
```

92

```
    res.json(user);
});


// Create new user (Create)
app.post('/users', (req, res) => {
    const { name } = req.body;
    const newUser = { id: users.length + 1, name
};
    users.push(newUser);
    res.status(201).json(newUser);
});


// Update user (Update)
app.put('/users/:id', (req, res) => {
    const user = users.find(u => u.id ===
parseInt(req.params.id));
    if (!user) return res.status(404).send('User
not found');

    user.name = req.body.name;
    res.json(user);
});


// Delete user (Delete)
app.delete('/users/:id', (req, res) => {
    const userIndex = users.findIndex(u => u.id
=== parseInt(req.params.id));
    if    (userIndex    ===    -1)    return
res.status(404).send('User not found');
```

```
    users.splice(userIndex, 1);
    res.status(204).send();
});

// Start the server
app.listen(port, () => {
    console.log(`Server           running           at
http://localhost:${port}/`);
});
```

Step 2: Test the API

1. **GET /users**: Retrieves all users.

   ```bash
   bash
   ```

   ```
   curl http://localhost:3000/users
   ```

2. **GET /users/:id**: Retrieves a specific user by ID.

   ```bash
   bash
   ```

   ```
   curl http://localhost:3000/users/1
   ```

3. **POST /users**: Creates a new user (send JSON data with name).

   ```bash
   bash
   ```

```
curl -X POST http://localhost:3000/users -
H  "Content-Type:  application/json"  -d
'{"name": "Alice Cooper"}'
```

4. **PUT /users/:id**: Updates an existing user.

```bash
```

```
curl  -X  PUT  http://localhost:3000/users/2
-H  "Content-Type:  application/json"  -d
'{"name": "Updated User"}'
```

5. **DELETE /users/:id**: Deletes a user by ID.

```bash
```

```
curl              -X              DELETE
http://localhost:3000/users/1
```

Conclusion

In this chapter, we introduced **Express.js**, explored how to set up an Express server, and discussed routing and middleware in Express. We also built a simple **RESTful API** to perform CRUD operations using Express. Express.js simplifies web development in Node.js, enabling developers to build powerful web applications and APIs with minimal effort.

In the next chapter, we'll dive deeper into handling advanced routing and creating more complex APIs using **Express.js**.

CHAPTER 8

HANDLING REQUESTS AND RESPONSES IN NODE.JS

Handling HTTP requests and responses is one of the fundamental tasks when building web applications or APIs. In this chapter, we will cover the core aspects of handling requests and responses in **Node.js** with **Express.js**, including various HTTP request methods (GET, POST, PUT, DELETE), working with request parameters and body parsing, creating dynamic responses, and error handling. We'll also provide a real-world example of building a **Form Submission API** using Express.

HTTP Request Methods (GET, POST, PUT, DELETE)

HTTP methods define the action to be performed on a resource. In Express.js, these methods map to route handlers that process incoming requests and return the appropriate response.

GET Method

The **GET** method is used to retrieve data from the server. It is the most common HTTP method and is typically used for reading or querying resources.

javascript

```
app.get('/users', (req, res) => {
    res.send('GET request to fetch all users');
});
```

POST Method

The **POST** method is used to send data to the server to create a new resource. It is commonly used for form submissions or creating new entries in a database.

javascript

```
app.post('/users', (req, res) => {
    res.send('POST request to create a new user');
});
```

PUT Method

The **PUT** method is used to update an existing resource on the server. It typically replaces the current resource with the new data provided.

javascript

```
app.put('/users/:id', (req, res) => {
    const userId = req.params.id;
    res.send(`PUT request to update user with ID
${userId}`);
});
```

DELETE Method

The **DELETE** method is used to remove a resource from the server.

javascript

```
app.delete('/users/:id', (req, res) => {
    const userId = req.params.id;
    res.send(`DELETE request to remove user with
ID ${userId}`);
});
```

Request Parameters and Body Parsing

Express allows you to handle request parameters, query strings, and the request body to build dynamic routes and perform actions based on user input.

Route Parameters

Route parameters are part of the URL and can be accessed using `req.params`. They are useful for handling dynamic data in the URL, such as user IDs or post IDs.

```javascript
app.get('/user/:id', (req, res) => {
    const userId = req.params.id;
    res.send(`User ID: ${userId}`);
});
```

In this example, `:id` is a route parameter, and its value is accessed via `req.params.id`.

Query Parameters

Query parameters are part of the URL after the ? symbol, and they are accessed using `req.query`. These are commonly used for filtering, pagination, or search.

```javascript
app.get('/search', (req, res) => {
    const { query, page } = req.query;
    res.send(`Search    query:    ${query},    Page
number: ${page}`);
});
```

In this example, `query` and `page` are query parameters, accessed via `req.query.query` and `req.query.page`.

Body Parsing

When receiving data from a form or client-side application (e.g., a POST or PUT request), you often need to parse the request body. Express uses middleware like **express.json()** and **express.urlencoded()** to handle this.

- **Parsing JSON bodies**:

    javascript

    ```
    app.use(express.json());    // Middleware
    for JSON body parsing
    ```

- **Parsing URL-encoded bodies (from HTML forms)**:

    javascript

    ```
    app.use(express.urlencoded({    extended:
    true }));    // Middleware for form data
    parsing
    ```

Example of handling POST data:

javascript

```
app.post('/submit', (req, res) => {
```

```
const { name, email } = req.body;
res.send(`Received data: Name = ${name},
Email = ${email}`);
});
```

Creating Dynamic Responses

Express makes it easy to create dynamic responses by rendering data, using templates, or sending back data in different formats such as JSON or HTML.

Sending JSON Responses

When building APIs, it is common to send JSON responses.

```
javascript
```

```
app.get('/api/user', (req, res) => {
    const user = { id: 1, name: 'John Doe', email:
'john@example.com' };
    res.json(user);
});
```

This will send a response with the `user` object in JSON format.

Rendering HTML Views with Templates

You can render HTML dynamically using templating engines like **EJS**, **Pug**, or **Handlebars**. First, install the required templating engine:

```
bash
```

```
npm install ejs --save
```

Then, set up the view engine in your Express app:

```
javascript
```

```
app.set('view engine', 'ejs');
```

Now you can render dynamic HTML pages:

```
javascript
```

```
app.get('/profile', (req, res) => {
    const user = { name: 'Alice', age: 25 };
    res.render('profile', { user });
});
```

This will render a `profile.ejs` template and pass the `user` object to it.

Error Handling with Express

Error handling is crucial for building reliable web applications. Express makes it easy to catch errors and send appropriate responses.

Basic Error Handling

In Express, errors are passed to the next middleware using `next(err)`.

Example:

```javascript
app.get('/error', (req, res, next) => {
    const err = new Error('Something went wrong!');
    err.status = 500;
    next(err);
});
```

Express also has a built-in error-handling middleware that you can use to catch and respond to errors globally:

```javascript
app.use((err, req, res, next) => {
    console.error(err.stack);
```

```
res.status(err.status                          ||
500).send('Something went wrong!');
});
```

Error Handling for Missing Routes

If a route doesn't match any of the defined routes, Express automatically returns a 404 response. You can customize this behavior:

```javascript
app.use((req, res) => {
    res.status(404).send('Route not found');
});
```

Real-World Example: A Form Submission API

Let's put everything we've learned together and build a simple **Form Submission API**. In this example, users will submit a form with their **name** and **email**, and the API will store the data (in memory) and send a response.

Step 1: Set Up the Express Server

First, install **Express.js** and set up the server:

```bash
bash
```

```
npm init -y
npm install express --save
```

Create a file called app.js:

```
javascript
```

```javascript
const express = require('express');
const app = express();
const port = 3000;

// Middleware for parsing form data
(application/x-www-form-urlencoded)
app.use(express.urlencoded({ extended: true }));

// Middleware for parsing JSON data
app.use(express.json());

// In-memory storage for form submissions
let submissions = [];

// POST route to handle form submissions
app.post('/submit-form', (req, res) => {
    const { name, email } = req.body;

    if (!name || !email) {
        return res.status(400).send('Name and
email are required');
    }
```

```
    // Save the data (in memory for this example)
    const submission = { name, email };
    submissions.push(submission);

    // Send back a success response
    res.status(200).json({
        message: 'Form submitted successfully',
        data: submission
    });
});

// GET route to fetch all submissions
app.get('/submissions', (req, res) => {
    res.json(submissions);
});

// Start the server
app.listen(port, () => {
    console.log(`Server          running          at
http://localhost:${port}`);
});
```

Step 2: Test the API

1. **Test Form Submission (POST)**: You can use **Postman** or **curl** to submit a form.

   Example using **curl**:

   bash

```
curl -X POST http://localhost:3000/submit-
form -H "Content-Type: application/x-www-
form-urlencoded"                        -d
"name=John&email=john@example.com"
```

Expected response:

```
json
```

```
{
  "message":         "Form         submitted
successfully",
  "data": {
    "name": "John",
    "email": "john@example.com"
  }
}
```

2. **Test Viewing Submissions (GET)**: To view all form submissions, use **curl** or your browser:

```
bash
```

```
curl http://localhost:3000/submissions
```

Expected response:

```
json
```

```
[
    {
        "name": "John",
        "email": "john@example.com"
    }
]
```

Conclusion

In this chapter, we covered the essential aspects of handling requests and responses in **Node.js** and **Express.js**. We explored the various HTTP request methods (GET, POST, PUT, DELETE), how to handle request parameters and parse request bodies, how to create dynamic responses, and how to implement error handling in your Express app.

We also built a real-world **Form Submission API** that accepts form data via POST requests and displays stored submissions. This example demonstrated how to handle user input, store it temporarily, and return a response using Express.

In the next chapter, we'll delve deeper into **middleware** in Express, focusing on how to use built-in middleware and custom middleware to handle various tasks like logging, authentication, and validation.

CHAPTER 9

BUILDING A RESTFUL API WITH EXPRESS

In this chapter, we will explore the concept of **REST (Representational State Transfer)** and how to build a **RESTful API** using **Express.js**. REST APIs are widely used for building scalable web applications and services, allowing clients to interact with server-side resources in a standardized way. We will cover the basics of REST, how to build routes for a REST API, handle JSON requests and responses, and perform CRUD (Create, Read, Update, Delete) operations. We will end the chapter with a real-world example of building a **Task Management API**.

What is REST and Why Use It?

REST (Representational State Transfer) is an architectural style for designing networked applications. It is widely used in web services and APIs due to its simplicity, scalability, and stateless nature.

Principles of REST:

1. **Stateless**: Each request from a client to a server must contain all the information the server needs to fulfill the request. The server does not store any session information between requests.

2. **Client-Server**: The client and server are separate entities. The client is responsible for the user interface and the server handles data storage and business logic.

3. **Uniform Interface**: RESTful APIs use standard HTTP methods (GET, POST, PUT, DELETE) for operations, which makes it easy to interact with the API.

4. **Resource-Based**: REST revolves around the concept of **resources**, which can be represented by URLs. A resource can be any data or object that the client can access or modify (e.g., user, task, product).

5. **Stateless Communication**: Each request is independent, and no information is retained between requests. Authentication and authorization are handled in each request, usually via headers (e.g., using tokens).

Why Use REST?

- **Simplicity**: RESTful APIs are easy to design and use. They leverage HTTP methods (GET, POST, PUT, DELETE) that are already familiar to most developers.

- **Scalability**: REST APIs can scale well because they follow the stateless principle, which means each request is independent and doesn't rely on previous ones.
- **Interoperability**: Since REST uses standard HTTP, it is platform-independent and can be consumed by a variety of clients, including web browsers, mobile apps, and other servers.

Building Routes for a REST API

In a RESTful API, you define routes to handle different HTTP requests for different resources. Each route is mapped to a specific HTTP method, which determines the action to be performed on the resource.

Here's how to define routes for common CRUD operations using Express.js:

GET Method (Read)

The **GET** method is used to retrieve information from the server.

```javascript
app.get('/tasks', (req, res) => {
    // Fetch and return all tasks
```

112

```
    res.json(tasks);  // Assuming 'tasks' is an
array of task objects
});
```

POST Method (Create)

The **POST** method is used to send data to the server and create a new resource.

```
javascript
```

```
app.post('/tasks', (req, res) => {
    const { name, description } = req.body;
    const newTask = { id: tasks.length + 1, name,
description };
    tasks.push(newTask);
    res.status(201).json(newTask);  // Return
the newly created task
});
```

PUT Method (Update)

The **PUT** method is used to update an existing resource.

```
javascript
```

```
app.put('/tasks/:id', (req, res) => {
    const taskId = parseInt(req.params.id);
    const task = tasks.find(t => t.id ===
taskId);
    if (!task) {
```

113

```
        return   res.status(404).send('Task   not
found');
    }
    task.name = req.body.name || task.name;
    task.description = req.body.description ||
task.description;
    res.json(task);   // Return the updated task
});
```

DELETE Method (Delete)

The **DELETE** method is used to remove a resource from the server.

javascript

```
app.delete('/tasks/:id', (req, res) => {
    const taskId = parseInt(req.params.id);
    const taskIndex = tasks.findIndex(t => t.id
=== taskId);
    if (taskIndex === -1) {
        return   res.status(404).send('Task   not
found');
    }
    tasks.splice(taskIndex, 1);   // Remove the
task from the array
    res.status(204).send(); // Send a no content
response
});
```

Handling JSON Requests and Responses

One of the key features of REST APIs is handling **JSON (JavaScript Object Notation)** data. Express makes it easy to handle JSON data using the built-in middleware **express.json()**, which parses incoming JSON request bodies.

Parsing JSON Data:

To parse JSON in incoming requests, add the following middleware:

javascript

```
app.use(express.json());  // Middleware to parse
JSON request bodies
```

Sending JSON Responses:

You can send JSON responses using the res.json() method:

javascript

```
app.get('/tasks', (req, res) => {
    res.json(tasks);  // Send the tasks as a JSON
response
});
```

CRUD Operations with Express

Let's now go through an example of performing **CRUD operations** with a simple in-memory task management system.

Step 1: Set Up the Express Server

Create a new file app.js and initialize an Express server:

javascript

```
const express = require('express');
const app = express();
const port = 3000;

app.use(express.json());  // Middleware to parse
JSON request bodies

let tasks = [
    { id: 1, name: 'Buy groceries', description:
'Milk, eggs, bread' },
    { id: 2, name: 'Complete homework',
description: 'Finish Node.js chapter' }
];

// GET route to fetch all tasks
app.get('/tasks', (req, res) => {
    res.json(tasks);
});
```

```javascript
// POST route to create a new task
app.post('/tasks', (req, res) => {
    const { name, description } = req.body;
    const newTask = { id: tasks.length + 1, name,
description };
    tasks.push(newTask);
    res.status(201).json(newTask);
});

// PUT route to update an existing task
app.put('/tasks/:id', (req, res) => {
    const taskId = parseInt(req.params.id);
    const task = tasks.find(t => t.id ===
taskId);
    if (!task) return res.status(404).send('Task
not found');
    task.name = req.body.name || task.name;
    task.description = req.body.description ||
task.description;
    res.json(task);
});

// DELETE route to remove a task
app.delete('/tasks/:id', (req, res) => {
    const taskId = parseInt(req.params.id);
    const taskIndex = tasks.findIndex(t => t.id
=== taskId);
```

```
    if    (taskIndex    ===    -1)    return
res.status(404).send('Task not found');
    tasks.splice(taskIndex, 1);
    res.status(204).send();
});


// Start the server
app.listen(port, () => {
    console.log(`Server          running          at
http://localhost:${port}`);
});
```

Step 2: Running the App

1. Start the server by running the following command:

   ```bash
   ```

   ```
   node app.js
   ```

2. Use **Postman** or **curl** to interact with the API.

- **GET /tasks**: Get a list of all tasks.

   ```bash
   ```

   ```
   curl http://localhost:3000/tasks
   ```

- **POST /tasks**: Create a new task.

   ```bash
   ```

```
curl -X POST http://localhost:3000/tasks -
H "Content-Type: application/json" -d
'{"name": "Go to the gym", "description":
"Leg day"}'
```

- **PUT /tasks/:id**: Update an existing task.

```bash
bash
```

```
curl -X PUT http://localhost:3000/tasks/2
-H "Content-Type: application/json" -d
'{"name": "Complete homework",
"description": "Finish Node.js chapter
with examples"}'
```

- **DELETE /tasks/:id**: Delete a task.

```bash
bash
```

```
curl -X DELETE
http://localhost:3000/tasks/1
```

Real-World Example: A Task Management API

In this real-world example, we've built a simple **Task Management API** using Express.js, where users can:

- **Create** a new task (POST /tasks).

- **Read** all tasks (GET /tasks).
- **Update** a task (PUT /tasks/:id).
- **Delete** a task (DELETE /tasks/:id).

This API demonstrates how to handle CRUD operations using REST principles, as well as how to manage JSON data in requests and responses.

Conclusion

In this chapter, we covered how to build a **RESTful API** with **Express.js**, focusing on routing, handling HTTP requests (GET, POST, PUT, DELETE), parsing JSON data, and performing CRUD operations. We also built a real-world example of a **Task Management API** to demonstrate these concepts in action.

In the next chapter, we will dive deeper into **middleware** and how to use it for tasks like authentication, logging, and error handling in your Express applications.

CHAPTER 10

WORKING WITH DATABASES IN NODE.JS

In this chapter, we'll explore how to connect a **Node.js** application to databases. We will discuss the differences between **SQL** (relational) and **NoSQL** (non-relational) databases, and how to work with **MongoDB** (a NoSQL database) using **Mongoose**, and **MySQL** (a relational database) in Node.js. Additionally, we'll cover the importance of **data validation** and **error handling** when working with databases. Finally, we'll build a **real-world blog app** that connects to **MongoDB** to store and retrieve data.

Introduction to Databases (SQL vs NoSQL)

Before diving into connecting databases with Node.js, it's important to understand the difference between **SQL** and **NoSQL** databases, as each has its strengths and use cases.

SQL (Relational) Databases:

- **Structure**: SQL databases are based on a **structured** data model with **tables**, **rows**, and **columns**. Data is stored in a tabular format.
- **Examples**: MySQL, PostgreSQL, SQLite.
- **Query Language**: SQL (Structured Query Language) is used for querying and managing data.
- **Use Case**: SQL databases are typically used when data is highly structured and relationships between entities (like tables) are important. They are often used for applications requiring ACID (Atomicity, Consistency, Isolation, Durability) transactions, such as banking systems and customer relationship management (CRM) systems.

NoSQL (Non-Relational) Databases:

- **Structure**: NoSQL databases use various data models, such as **documents**, **key-value pairs**, **wide-column stores**, or **graphs**. Data is often **unstructured** or **semi-structured**.
- **Examples**: MongoDB, CouchDB, Cassandra, Redis.
- **Query Language**: NoSQL databases often do not use SQL. Instead, they use their own query languages or APIs.
- **Use Case**: NoSQL databases are great for applications requiring high scalability and flexibility. They are

122

commonly used for real-time applications, social media platforms, and data with rapidly changing or semi-structured schemas (e.g., e-commerce platforms).

Choosing Between SQL and NoSQL:

- Use **SQL** when your data is structured with well-defined relationships, such as when you need to enforce complex queries or transactions.
- Use **NoSQL** when your data is semi-structured, the schema might change over time, or when you need high scalability and fast reads/writes for large volumes of data.

Using MongoDB with Mongoose in Node.js

MongoDB is a NoSQL database that stores data in **JSON-like documents** called **BSON** (Binary JSON). Mongoose is an **Object Data Modeling (ODM)** library for MongoDB and Node.js, which provides a higher-level abstraction for working with MongoDB.

Step 1: Install MongoDB and Mongoose

To use MongoDB in your Node.js project, you first need to install **Mongoose** via npm:

bash

```
npm install mongoose --save
```

You will also need to have **MongoDB** installed locally or use a cloud-based instance like **MongoDB Atlas**.

Step 2: Connect to MongoDB with Mongoose

To connect to MongoDB, you need to import Mongoose and call the `connect()` method. This method establishes a connection to your database.

```javascript
const mongoose = require('mongoose');

// Connect to MongoDB
mongoose.connect('mongodb://localhost/blog-app', { useNewUrlParser: true, useUnifiedTopology: true })
  .then(() => {
    console.log('Connected to MongoDB');
  })
  .catch(err => {
    console.log('Error connecting to MongoDB:', err);
  });
```

In this example, the app connects to a local MongoDB instance. You can replace `'mongodb://localhost/blog-app'` with the connection string for **MongoDB Atlas** if you're using the cloud service.

Step 3: Create a Mongoose Model

A Mongoose **model** is a wrapper around a MongoDB collection. It allows you to define schemas (the structure of the documents) and interact with MongoDB through a simpler API.

```javascript
const mongoose = require('mongoose');

// Define a schema for a blog post
const postSchema = new mongoose.Schema({
    title: { type: String, required: true },
    content: { type: String, required: true },
    author: { type: String, required: true },
    date: { type: Date, default: Date.now }
});

// Create a model based on the schema
const Post = mongoose.model('Post', postSchema);
```

In this example, we define a **Post** model with title, content, author, and date fields.

Step 4: Create a New Document

You can now create a new blog post by creating an instance of the **Post** model and saving it to MongoDB.

```javascript
const newPost = new Post({
    title: 'My First Blog Post',
    content: 'This is the content of my first
post.',
    author: 'John Doe'
});

newPost.save()
    .then(post => {
        console.log('Post saved:', post);
    })
    .catch(err => {
        console.log('Error saving post:', err);
    });
```

Connecting a Node.js App to MySQL

Next, let's look at how to connect your **Node.js** app to a **MySQL** database.

Step 1: Install MySQL and mysql2

You can use the `mysql2` package to connect your Node.js app to MySQL. Install it via npm:

```bash
npm install mysql2 --save
```

Step 2: Create a Connection to MySQL

Once installed, you can use the `mysql2` package to connect to your MySQL database.

```javascript
const mysql = require('mysql2');

// Create a connection to the MySQL database
const connection = mysql.createConnection({
    host: 'localhost',
    user: 'root',
    password: '',
    database: 'blog_app'
});

// Connect to MySQL
connection.connect(err => {
    if (err) {
```

```
      console.error('Error    connecting    to
MySQL:', err);
      return;
  }
  console.log('Connected to MySQL');
});
```

Replace `localhost`, `root`, and the database name (`blog_app`) with your own credentials.

Step 3: Create and Query the Database

After connecting to MySQL, you can create tables and run queries.

Example of creating a table:

```javascript

const createTableQuery = `
CREATE TABLE IF NOT EXISTS posts (
    id INT AUTO_INCREMENT PRIMARY KEY,
    title VARCHAR(255) NOT NULL,
    content TEXT NOT NULL,
    author VARCHAR(255) NOT NULL,
    date TIMESTAMP DEFAULT CURRENT_TIMESTAMP
);
`;
```

```
connection.query(createTableQuery,        (err,
results) => {
    if (err) {
        console.log('Error    creating    table:',
err);
    } else {
        console.log('Table   created   or   already
exists');
    }
});
```

Example of querying data:

```
javascript
```

```
connection.query('SELECT  *  FROM  posts', (err,
results) => {
    if (err) {
        console.log('Error    querying    posts:',
err);
    } else {
        console.log('Posts:', results);
    }
});
```

Data Validation and Error Handling in Databases

Data validation is crucial when working with databases to ensure that the data you're inserting or updating follows the correct structure and types.

Mongoose Validation

Mongoose allows you to define validation rules on schema fields. For example:

```javascript
const postSchema = new mongoose.Schema({
    title: {
        type: String,
        required: true,
        minlength: [5, 'Title must be at least 5 characters long']
    },
    content: {
        type: String,
        required: true
    },
    author: {
        type: String,
        required: true
    }
});
```

This schema ensures that a **title** is required and must be at least 5 characters long, and **content** and **author** must be present.

Error Handling in MySQL

In MySQL, you should always handle errors in your queries to ensure that you can catch issues like invalid data or connection problems.

Example of handling errors:

```javascript
connection.query('INSERT INTO posts (title, content, author) VALUES (?, ?, ?)', ['My Post', 'This is the content', 'John Doe'], (err, results) => {
    if (err) {
        console.log('Error inserting data:', err);
    } else {
        console.log('Data inserted:', results);
    }
});
```

Real-World Example: Connecting a Blog App to MongoDB

Let's build a real-world example where we connect a simple **blog app** to MongoDB and perform CRUD operations.

Step 1: Set Up the Express Server
javascript

```
const express = require('express');
const mongoose = require('mongoose');
const app = express();
const port = 3000;

app.use(express.json());    // Middleware for
parsing JSON request bodies

// Connect to MongoDB
mongoose.connect('mongodb://localhost/blog-
app',        {        useNewUrlParser:        true,
useUnifiedTopology: true })
  .then(()    =>    console.log('Connected    to
MongoDB'))
  .catch(err => console.log('Error connecting to
MongoDB:', err));

// Define the Post schema and model
const postSchema = new mongoose.Schema({
    title: { type: String, required: true },
    content: { type: String, required: true },
```

```
    author: { type: String, required: true },
    date: { type: Date, default: Date.now }
});


const Post = mongoose.model('Post', postSchema);

// POST route to create a new blog post
app.post('/posts', (req, res) => {
    const { title, content, author } = req.body;
    const newPost = new Post({ title, content,
author });

    newPost.save()
        .then(post                              =>
res.status(201).json(post))
        .catch(err                              =>
res.status(400).send('Error   creating   post:',
err));
});

// GET route to fetch all posts
app.get('/posts', (req, res) => {
    Post.find()
        .then(posts => res.json(posts))
        .catch(err                              =>
res.status(400).send('Error   fetching   posts:',
err));
});
```

```
// Start the server
app.listen(port, () => {
    console.log(`Server          running          at
http://localhost:${port}`);
});
```

Step 2: Running the App

1. Start the MongoDB server (if using local MongoDB):

    bash

    ```
    mongod
    ```

2. Start the Node.js server:

    bash

    ```
    node app.js
    ```

3. Use **Postman** or **curl** to test the API:

    -   **POST /posts**: Create a new blog post.

    bash

    ```
    curl -X POST http://localhost:3000/posts -
    H "Content-Type: application/json" -d
    '{"title": "My first blog", "content":
    "This is my first post!", "author":
    "John"}'
    ```

134

- **GET /posts**: Get a list of all posts.

```bash
bash
```

```bash
curl http://localhost:3000/posts
```

Conclusion

In this chapter, we covered how to connect **Node.js** applications to **MongoDB** and **MySQL** databases. We also explored the importance of data validation and error handling when interacting with databases. Finally, we built a real-world **Blog App** that connects to **MongoDB**, where we performed **CRUD operations** for creating and fetching blog posts.

In the next chapter, we'll explore **authentication** in Node.js and how to secure APIs and user data effectively.

CHAPTER 11

AUTHENTICATION AND AUTHORIZATION IN NODE.JS

In this chapter, we will explore the concepts of **authentication** and **authorization** in Node.js. These concepts are essential for securing web applications and ensuring that only authorized users can access specific resources. We'll discuss the difference between **session-based** and **token-based** authentication, focus on **JWT (JSON Web Tokens)** as a token-based approach, and introduce **Passport.js**, a popular middleware for handling authentication in Node.js applications. Finally, we will build a **secure login system** for a web app using **JWT**.

Session vs. Token-Based Authentication

Authentication is the process of verifying the identity of a user, while authorization is the process of granting or denying access to resources based on the user's identity.

Session-Based Authentication

In **session-based authentication**, the server stores user session information, typically in memory or a database. When a user logs in, the server creates a **session ID** and stores it on the server, often in a session store or a database. This session ID is then sent to the user's browser in the form of a **cookie**.

1. The user sends a request with the session ID in the cookie.
2. The server retrieves the session from the session store and authenticates the user.
3. If the session is valid, the server authorizes the request.

While session-based authentication is simple and secure for server-side rendered applications, it may not be suitable for distributed systems, as managing sessions across multiple servers or instances can be complex.

Token-Based Authentication (JWT)

Token-based authentication is more modern and works well for distributed and stateless applications. Instead of storing session data on the server, a token (usually a **JWT**) is generated and sent to the client after successful login. This token contains all the information needed to authenticate and authorize the user.

1. The user logs in and the server generates a JWT.

2. The JWT is sent to the client and stored (usually in local storage or a cookie).

3. On subsequent requests, the client sends the JWT in the **Authorization** header.

4. The server verifies the token and authorizes the user.

JWT tokens are **stateless** and are often used in APIs and single-page applications (SPAs) because they don't require server-side session storage.

Using JWT (JSON Web Tokens)

JSON Web Tokens (JWT) are a compact, URL-safe means of representing claims to be transferred between two parties. JWTs consist of three parts:

1. **Header**: Contains metadata about the token (e.g., the signing algorithm).

2. **Payload**: Contains the claims or data, typically user information like ID, username, and roles.

3. **Signature**: Ensures the token's authenticity and integrity. It's created by signing the header and payload with a secret key.

138

Step 1: Installing Required Packages

To use JWT in a Node.js application, you need to install the **jsonwebtoken** package:

```bash
bash
```

```bash
npm install jsonwebtoken --save
```

Step 2: Generating a JWT Token

After a user successfully logs in, you can generate a JWT token as follows:

```javascript
javascript
```

```javascript
const jwt = require('jsonwebtoken');

// User information to be encoded into the token
const user = {
    id: 1,
    username: 'johndoe'
};

// Secret key for signing the token (should be
stored securely)
const secretKey = 'your-secret-key';

// Generate the token
```

```
const token = jwt.sign(user, secretKey, {
expiresIn: '1h' });
```

```
console.log('Generated JWT:', token);
```

The expiresIn option specifies the lifetime of the token (in this case, 1 hour).

Step 3: Verifying JWT Token

When the user sends the token in the **Authorization** header, the server can verify the token to ensure its authenticity:

javascript

```
const jwt = require('jsonwebtoken');
```

```
const token =
req.headers['authorization'].split(' ')[1];   //
Bearer token
```

```
jwt.verify(token, secretKey, (err, decoded) => {
    if (err) {
        return res.status(401).send('Invalid or
expired token');
    }

    // Access decoded data (e.g., user info)
    console.log(decoded);   // { id: 1, username:
'johndoe' }
```

140

```
    // Proceed with request processing
});
```

In this example, the token is extracted from the **Authorization** header, and `jwt.verify()` is used to check the token's validity. If the token is valid, the request is allowed to proceed.

Passport.js for Authentication

Passport.js is a powerful and flexible authentication middleware for Node.js. It supports over 500 authentication strategies (such as OAuth, OpenID, and local authentication) and integrates easily with Express.js.

Step 1: Installing Passport.js

First, you need to install **Passport.js** and some related packages:

```bash
npm install passport passport-local express-
session --save
```

- **passport-local**: A strategy for username/password authentication.
- **express-session**: For managing user sessions.

141

Step 2: Setting Up Passport.js

Here's how to set up **Passport.js** for local authentication using a simple username/password strategy:

1. **Initialize Passport and Session Middleware**:

javascript

```
const express = require('express');
const passport = require('passport');
const LocalStrategy = require('passport-local').Strategy;
const session = require('express-session');
const app = express();

app.use(express.json());
app.use(session({ secret: 'your-secret-key',
resave: false, saveUninitialized: true }));
app.use(passport.initialize());
app.use(passport.session());
```

2. **Configure the Local Strategy**:

javascript

```
passport.use(new LocalStrategy((username,
password, done) => {
    // Simulate a user lookup (you would
typically query the database here)
```

```
    if (username === 'johndoe' && password ===
'password123') {
        return done(null, { id: 1, username:
'johndoe' });
    } else {
        return done(null, false, { message:
'Invalid credentials' });
    }
}));


// Serialize and deserialize user information for
session management
passport.serializeUser((user,      done)      =>
done(null, user.id));
passport.deserializeUser((id,      done)      =>
done(null, { id, username: 'johndoe' }));
```

3. Create Login Route:

javascript

```
app.post('/login',
passport.authenticate('local', {
    successRedirect: '/dashboard',
    failureRedirect: '/login',
    failureFlash: true
}));
```

4. **Secure Routes with Authentication**: Use `passport.authenticate()` to protect routes and ensure users are authenticated before accessing them:

javascript

```javascript
app.get('/dashboard', (req, res) => {
    if (req.isAuthenticated()) {
        res.send('Welcome to the dashboard');
    } else {
        res.redirect('/login');
    }
});
```

Real-World Example: Secure Login for a Web App

Let's put everything we've learned together and build a simple **login system** using **JWT** for authentication.

Step 1: Setting Up the Express Server

First, initialize the project and install required packages:

bash

```bash
npm init -y
npm install express jsonwebtoken bcryptjs --save
```

Create a file called `app.js`:

144

```javascript
const express = require('express');
const jwt = require('jsonwebtoken');
const bcrypt = require('bcryptjs');
const app = express();
const port = 3000;

app.use(express.json());

// User data (in-memory storage for this example)
const users = [
    { id: 1, username: 'johndoe', password:
'$2a$10$H6eYM5C7YPiGG.zJGrV3gEqMcjtTtF1fJ6O8JxO
Fl21aQwTtDGo7u' }  // 'password123' hashed
];

// JWT secret key
const secretKey = 'your-secret-key';

// Login route
app.post('/login', (req, res) => {
    const { username, password } = req.body;

    const user = users.find(u => u.username ===
username);
    if              (!user)              return
res.status(401).send('Invalid credentials');
```

```
    bcrypt.compare(password,      user.password,
(err, isMatch) => {
        if (err) throw err;
        if          (!isMatch)          return
res.status(401).send('Invalid credentials');

        const token = jwt.sign({ id: user.id,
username:    user.username   },    secretKey,    {
expiresIn: '1h' });
        res.json({ token });
    });
});

// Protected route
app.get('/profile', (req, res) => {
    const            token            =
req.headers['authorization']?.split(' ')[1];  //
Bearer <token>

    if            (!token)            return
res.status(401).send('Access    denied,    token
missing');

    jwt.verify(token, secretKey, (err, decoded)
=> {
        if            (err)            return
res.status(401).send('Invalid    or    expired
token');
```

```
      res.json({ message: 'Welcome  to  your
profile', user: decoded });
    });
});

app.listen(port, () => {
    console.log(`Server        running        at
http://localhost:${port}`);
});
```

In this example:

- **Login Route (/login)**: Accepts username and password, verifies the credentials, and returns a JWT token.
- **Profile Route (/profile)**: Protects the route with JWT authentication. Users must provide a valid token to access the profile.

Step 2: Running the App

1. **Start the server**:

```
bash

node app.js
```

2. **Test the login** using **Postman** or **curl**.
   - o **POST /login**:

```bash
bash
```

```bash
curl              -X              POST
http://localhost:3000/login      -H
"Content-Type: application/json" -d
'{"username": "johndoe", "password":
"password123"}'
```

3. This will return a JWT token.

    o **GET /profile**: Use the token received from the
       login route and pass it in the **Authorization**
       header (e.g., `Bearer <token>`).

Conclusion

In this chapter, we covered how to implement **authentication** and
authorization in Node.js applications using **JWT** and
Passport.js. We discussed the difference between **session-based**
and **token-based authentication** and how to create a **secure login
system** with JWT. We also explored how to protect routes and
manage user sessions in a web app.

In the next chapter, we will dive into **middleware** and **advanced
error handling** techniques in Express.js to build more robust and
secure web applications.

CHAPTER 12

USING WEBSOCKETS FOR REAL-TIME APPLICATIONS

In this chapter, we will explore how to implement **real-time communication** in your web applications using **WebSockets**. We'll introduce the concept of WebSockets, explain how to set up **Socket.IO** (a popular library for WebSocket communication in Node.js), and walk you through building a **real-time chat application**. We will also cover **event handling** and **broadcasting** in real-time communication. To solidify the concepts, we'll build a **live chat feature** as a real-world example.

Understanding WebSockets

WebSockets provide full-duplex, bidirectional communication channels over a single, long-lived connection. Unlike traditional HTTP communication, which is request-response-based (client sends a request, server sends a response), WebSockets allow for continuous communication without the need for repeated requests.

Key Features of WebSockets:

- **Low Latency**: WebSockets provide instant communication with minimal delay, making them ideal for real-time applications like chat apps, notifications, and gaming.
- **Bidirectional Communication**: Both the server and the client can send and receive data independently. This is in contrast to HTTP, where the client always initiates the request.
- **Persistent Connection**: The WebSocket connection remains open until closed by either the client or the server, reducing the overhead of creating new connections for every request.

Use Cases for WebSockets:

- **Real-time chat applications**
- **Live updates (e.g., stock prices, social media feeds)**
- **Online multiplayer games**
- **Collaborative tools (e.g., Google Docs)**

Setting Up Socket.IO for Real-Time Communication

Socket.IO is a popular library for **real-time communication** in Node.js, which uses WebSockets under the hood but also provides fallback options for clients that don't support WebSockets (e.g., older browsers). Socket.IO is easy to set up and manage in Express applications.

Step 1: Installing Socket.IO

Start by installing **Socket.IO** in your project:

```bash
npm install socket.io --save
```

Step 2: Setting Up the Server

After installing Socket.IO, set up the server by integrating it with your Express app. Here's how you can set up a basic **Socket.IO** server:

```javascript
const express = require('express');
const http = require('http');
const socketIo = require('socket.io');

// Create an Express app
const app = express();

// Create a HTTP server
const server = http.createServer(app);
```

```
// Set up Socket.IO on the server
const io = socketIo(server);

// Serve static files (optional)
app.use(express.static('public'));

// Start the server
server.listen(3000, () => {
  console.log('Server          running          at
http://localhost:3000');
});
```

In this setup:

- **Express** is used to handle HTTP requests.
- **http** creates a server instance that is passed to Socket.IO.
- **Socket.IO** is initialized using the `socketIo` function, passing in the server.

Building a Real-Time Chat Application

Let's build a simple real-time chat application where users can send and receive messages in real-time.

Step 1: Setting Up the Frontend (Client-side)

Create an `index.html` file inside the `public` folder to serve the chat interface:

html

```
<!DOCTYPE html>
<html lang="en">
<head>
    <meta charset="UTF-8">
    <meta name="viewport" content="width=device-width, initial-scale=1.0">
    <title>Real-Time Chat App</title>
    <script src="/socket.io/socket.io.js"></script>
    <style>
        body {
            font-family: Arial, sans-serif;
            padding: 20px;
        }
        #messages {
            max-height: 300px;
            overflow-y: scroll;
        }
        .message {
            padding: 10px;
            background-color: #f0f0f0;
            margin-bottom: 5px;
            border-radius: 5px;
        }
        input {
            padding: 10px;
            width: 80%;
```

```
            border-radius: 5px;
            border: 1px solid #ccc;
        }
        button {
            padding: 10px;
            border: 1px solid #ccc;
            background-color: #28a745;
            color: white;
            border-radius: 5px;
        }
    </style>
</head>
<body>
    <h1>Real-Time Chat</h1>
    <div id="messages"></div>
    <input    id="messageInput"    type="text"
placeholder="Type a message...">
    <button
onclick="sendMessage()">Send</button>

    <script>
        const socket = io();

        // Listen for new messages
        socket.on('message', (data) => {
            const        messagesDiv        =
document.getElementById('messages');
            const        messageElement        =
document.createElement('div');
```

```
        messageElement.className          =
'message';
        messageElement.innerText = data;

messagesDiv.appendChild(messageElement);
        messagesDiv.scrollTop          =
messagesDiv.scrollHeight;
    });


    // Send message to server
    function sendMessage() {
        const          messageInput          =
document.getElementById('messageInput');
        const message = messageInput.value;
        socket.emit('send_message',
message); // Emit a 'send_message' event
        messageInput.value = ''; // Clear the
input field
    }
  </script>
</body>
</html>
```

In the above HTML:

- **Socket.IO client library** is included via the `<script src="/socket.io/socket.io.js">` tag.

- The messages div will display incoming chat messages, and users can input a message and send it by clicking the button.

Step 2: Setting Up the Backend (Server-side)

Now, let's update the **server** to listen for events from the client and broadcast the messages to all connected clients.

Update your app.js file to include event handling:

javascript

```
const express = require('express');
const http = require('http');
const socketIo = require('socket.io');

const app = express();
const server = http.createServer(app);
const io = socketIo(server);

// Serve static files
app.use(express.static('public'));

// Handle new connections
io.on('connection', (socket) => {
    console.log('A user connected');

    // Listen for incoming messages
```

```
socket.on('send_message', (message) => {
    // Broadcast message to all clients
    io.emit('message', message);
});


// Handle disconnections
socket.on('disconnect', () => {
    console.log('A user disconnected');
});
});


// Start the server
server.listen(3000, () => {
    console.log('Server          running          at
http://localhost:3000');
});
```

Here's what's happening:

- **io.on('connection', (socket) => {...})**:
  When a new client connects, this event is triggered, and
  we can set up the communication.

- **socket.on('send_message', (message) =>
  {...})**: When a message is received from the client, we
  broadcast it to all connected clients using
  io.emit('message', message).

Handling Events and Broadcasting in Real-Time

In the above example, **broadcasting** is accomplished using `io.emit()`, which sends a message to all connected clients. You can also target specific clients by using `socket.emit()` to send a message to just the client that initiated the event.

Broadcast to All Clients Except the Sender

Sometimes, you might want to broadcast a message to all clients except the sender. You can achieve this by using `socket.broadcast.emit()`:

javascript

```javascript
socket.on('send_message', (message) => {
    socket.broadcast.emit('message',  message);
// Broadcast to all clients except the sender
});
```

Handling Different Types of Events

Socket.IO supports custom events that you can use to define specific communication channels between the client and the server. You can also use namespaces and rooms for more complex applications.

158

Real-World Example: Building a Live Chat Feature

In the previous sections, we demonstrated how to build a simple chat application using **WebSockets** with **Socket.IO**. Let's recap the process and explore how we can add more features to the chat system:

1. **Real-Time Messaging**: With **Socket.IO**, messages are instantly broadcasted to all clients connected to the server, making the chat real-time.

2. **Event Handling**: We handle different events like `send_message` and `message`, allowing us to define clear communication between the client and server.

3. **Broadcasting**: Socket.IO's `emit()` and `broadcast.emit()` methods allow us to manage how messages are sent to multiple clients.

You can extend this example by adding:

- User authentication (e.g., using **JWT** for verifying users).
- Storing chat history in a database (e.g., **MongoDB** or **MySQL**).
- Implementing private messages or rooms.

159

Conclusion

In this chapter, we explored how to use **WebSockets** for real-time communication in Node.js applications. We covered the basics of **WebSockets**, how to set up **Socket.IO** in Node.js, and how to build a **real-time chat application**. Additionally, we discussed handling events, broadcasting messages to multiple clients, and building more interactive features for your web apps.

In the next chapter, we'll dive into **deploying** your Node.js applications and discuss best practices for scaling, monitoring, and maintaining real-time applications in production.

CHAPTER 13

ASYNCHRONOUS PROGRAMMING IN NODE.JS

In Node.js, **asynchronous programming** is a fundamental concept due to its non-blocking nature, allowing the application to handle multiple tasks concurrently. In this chapter, we will discuss different approaches to handling asynchronous operations in Node.js, such as **callbacks**, **promises**, and **async/await**. We will also work through a real-world example to illustrate how asynchronous code is used in a Node.js web application.

Callbacks and Callback Hell

What are Callbacks?

A **callback** is a function that is passed as an argument to another function and is executed after the completion of that function's operation. In Node.js, callbacks are commonly used for asynchronous operations, like reading files, making network requests, or querying databases.

Here's an example of a simple callback function:

```
javascript
```

```javascript
function fetchData(callback) {
    setTimeout(() => {
        console.log('Data fetched');
        callback();
    }, 2000);
}

fetchData(() => {
    console.log('Callback executed after data is
fetched');
});
```

In the example above, `fetchData` takes a `callback` function and executes it once the asynchronous operation (simulated with `setTimeout`) is complete.

Callback Hell

A common issue with using callbacks extensively is that it can lead to **callback hell**—a situation where callbacks are nested within other callbacks, creating a deeply indented and hard-to-read code structure.

Here's an example of callback hell:

```
javascript
```

```
function fetchData(callback) {
    setTimeout(() => {
        console.log('Data fetched');
        callback(null, 'Some data');
    }, 2000);
}

function processData(data, callback) {
    setTimeout(() => {
        console.log('Processing data');
        callback(null, 'Processed data');
    }, 2000);
}

function saveData(data, callback) {
    setTimeout(() => {
        console.log('Saving data');
        callback(null, 'Data saved');
    }, 2000);
}

// Callback Hell
fetchData((err, data) => {
    if (err) return console.error(err);
    processData(data, (err, processedData) => {
        if (err) return console.error(err);
        saveData(processedData, (err, result) =>
{
        if (err) return console.error(err);
```

```
        console.log(result);
    });
  });
});
```

In this example, the code becomes increasingly difficult to follow as more nested callbacks are added. This is what we call **callback hell**.

Promises and Chainable Asynchronous Code

What is a Promise?

A **promise** is an object representing the eventual completion or failure of an asynchronous operation. Promises allow you to write asynchronous code in a more structured and readable way, avoiding callback hell. A promise has three states:

- **Pending**: The initial state, neither fulfilled nor rejected.
- **Fulfilled**: The operation completed successfully.
- **Rejected**: The operation failed.

Creating a Promise

You can create a promise using the `new Promise()` constructor:

javascript

```
function fetchData() {
    return new Promise((resolve, reject) => {
        setTimeout(() => {
            console.log('Data fetched');
            resolve('Some data');
        }, 2000);
    });
}

fetchData().then((data) => {
    console.log(data);  // 'Some data'
}).catch((err) => {
    console.error(err);
});
```

In the example above, we use the `resolve()` function to fulfill the promise, and `reject()` to reject it in case of an error.

Chaining Promises

One of the main advantages of promises is that they can be **chained**, making it easier to handle multiple asynchronous operations sequentially:

```
javascript

fetchData()
    .then((data) => {
        console.log('Processing data');
```

165

```
        return 'Processed data';  // Return a new
promise or value
    })
    .then((processedData) => {
        console.log('Saving data');
        return 'Data saved';  // Return another
promise or value
    })
    .then((result) => {
        console.log(result);  // 'Data saved'
    })
    .catch((err) => {
        console.error(err);  // Handle errors
    });
```

In this example, each `.then()` function returns a promise, and you can chain multiple asynchronous operations together.

Async/Await in Node.js

What is Async/Await?

Async/await is a more modern and cleaner way of handling asynchronous code in Node.js. It is built on top of promises and makes asynchronous code look and behave more like synchronous code, improving readability and reducing nesting.

- **async**: A function is declared as asynchronous using the `async` keyword. An `async` function always returns a promise.
- **await**: The `await` keyword is used inside `async` functions to wait for a promise to resolve or reject. The code execution pauses at `await` until the promise is settled, making it appear synchronous.

Creating Async Functions

Here's how to convert the promise-based code to `async/await`:

javascript

```
async function fetchData() {
    return new Promise((resolve, reject) => {
        setTimeout(() => {
            console.log('Data fetched');
            resolve('Some data');
        }, 2000);
    });
}

async function processData() {
    const data = await fetchData();
    console.log(data);  // 'Some data'
}

processData();
```

Handling Errors with Async/Await

You can handle errors using a `try...catch` block within `async` functions:

javascript

```javascript
async function fetchData() {
    return new Promise((resolve, reject) => {
        setTimeout(() => {
            console.log('Data fetched');
            reject('Failed to fetch data');
        }, 2000);
    });
}

async function processData() {
    try {
        const data = await fetchData();
        console.log(data);
    } catch (error) {
        console.error(error);    // 'Failed to
fetch data'
    }
}

processData();
```

In this example, if the promise is rejected, the `catch` block will handle the error.

Real-World Example: Async API Calls in a Web App

Now let's implement a real-world example where we use **async/await** and **promises** to make **API calls** in a Node.js web application. We'll simulate calling two APIs to fetch user data and posts for a given user.

Step 1: Install Dependencies

For this example, we'll use the `axios` library to make HTTP requests. Install `axios` using npm:

```bash
npm install axios --save
```

Step 2: Create the Async API Calls

```javascript
const axios = require('axios');

// Fetch user data
async function getUserData(userId) {
```

```
  const          response          =          await
axios.get(`https://jsonplaceholder.typicode.com
/users/${userId}`);
    return response.data;
}


// Fetch posts for a user
async function getUserPosts(userId) {
    const          response          =          await
axios.get(`https://jsonplaceholder.typicode.com
/posts?userId=${userId}`);
    return response.data;
}


// Main function to fetch and display user data
and posts
async function displayUserData(userId) {
    try {
        const     userData     =          await
getUserData(userId);
        console.log('User Data:', userData);


        const     userPosts     =          await
getUserPosts(userId);
        console.log('User Posts:', userPosts);
    } catch (error) {
        console.error('Error   fetching   data:',
error);
    }
```

```
}
```

```
displayUserData(1);
```

In this example:

- We use **axios** to fetch data from a simulated API (jsonplaceholder.typicode.com).
- The getUserData and getUserPosts functions are async functions that return promises.
- The displayUserData function uses await to wait for the API calls to finish before displaying the data.

Step 3: Running the Application

1. Run the application with:

```bash
```

```
node app.js
```

2. The output should be:

```plaintext
```

```
User Data: { id: 1, name: 'Leanne Graham',
... }
```

171

```
User Posts: [ { id: 1, title: '...', body:
'...' }, { id: 2, title: '...', body: '...'
}, ... ]
```

Conclusion

In this chapter, we explored **asynchronous programming** in Node.js. We discussed how to handle asynchronous operations using **callbacks**, the issues with **callback hell**, and how to improve readability with **promises** and **async/await**. We also built a real-world example of making **async API calls** in a Node.js web application using **axios** and **async/await**.

Understanding asynchronous programming is key to writing efficient and scalable applications in Node.js. In the next chapter, we will explore **error handling** and **logging** techniques in Node.js to help you build more robust applications.

CHAPTER 14

ERROR HANDLING AND
DEBUGGING IN NODE.JS

In this chapter, we will explore error handling and debugging in **Node.js**. Handling errors effectively and debugging code are essential skills for building robust applications. We will cover the different types of errors in Node.js, how to use **try...catch** for synchronous and asynchronous code, and introduce some useful **debugging tools**. Finally, we will walk through a real-world example of **debugging an Express app**.

Types of Errors in Node.js

Node.js, being an asynchronous framework, uses a variety of error types, each with a specific purpose. Here are the most common error types:

1. System Errors

These errors are generated by the system (e.g., file system, network, or process errors). They usually arise from external factors and can be handled using error handling methods.

173

Example:

```
javascript

const fs = require('fs');

fs.readFile('nonexistent-file.txt', (err, data)
=> {
    if (err) {
        console.error('System            error:',
err.message);
    } else {
        console.log(data);
    }
});
```

2. Syntax Errors

These occur when there is a mistake in the JavaScript syntax itself, such as missing parentheses or commas. These are usually caught during development or when running the application.

Example:

```
javascript

// Syntax error: Missing closing parenthesis
console.log('Hello, world!';
```

3. Runtime Errors

These errors occur while the program is running. These can be due to various issues, such as undefined variables or operations that cannot be performed on a certain data type.

Example:

javascript

```javascript
let obj;
console.log(obj.property);   //  Runtime  error:
Cannot read property 'property' of undefined
```

4. Logical Errors

These errors don't throw any exceptions or crash the program but lead to incorrect behavior. Logical errors are harder to detect and fix because they don't produce immediate error messages.

Example:

javascript

```javascript
let sum = 0;
for (let i = 1; i < 10; i++) { // Should be i <=
10 to include 10
    sum += i;
}
```

```
console.log(sum); // Incorrect sum because of
logic error in the loop
```

Using try...catch for Synchronous Code

The **try...catch** statement is used to handle errors in synchronous code. It allows you to try a block of code and catch any errors that occur within it. This is particularly useful for handling runtime errors.

Basic Usage:

javascript

```
try {
    let result = riskyFunction(); // Might throw
an error
    console.log('Function            executed
successfully:', result);
} catch (err) {
    console.error('Error            occurred:',
err.message);
}
```

In the above example, the riskyFunction() might throw an error. If it does, the catch block will catch it, preventing the application from crashing.

Handling Specific Errors:

You can handle different types of errors by checking the error message or using **instanceof** to differentiate between error types.

javascript

```
try {
    const data = fs.readFileSync('nonexistent-
file.txt');
} catch (err) {
   if (err instanceof Error) {
       console.error('General            error:',
err.message);
    } else {
       console.error('Unknown error type');
    }
}
```

Handling Asynchronous Errors

Error handling in asynchronous code (such as callback-based functions or promises) requires a slightly different approach.

1. Using try...catch with Async/Await

If you are using **async/await**, you can wrap your asynchronous code in a try...catch block to handle errors.

```
javascript

async function fetchData() {
    try {
        const        response        =        await
fetch('https://example.com/api');
        const data = await response.json();
        console.log(data);
    } catch (error) {
        console.error('Error    fetching    data:',
error.message);
    }
}
```

In this example, any errors thrown by the `fetch` operation will be caught by the `catch` block.

2. Handling Errors with Promises

When working with **promises**, you can use `.catch()` to handle any errors.

```
javascript

fetch('https://example.com/api')
    .then(response => response.json())
    .then(data => console.log(data))
    .catch(err => console.error('Error   fetching
data:', err.message));
```

The .catch() method will handle any errors that occur during the promise chain.

3. Callback Error Handling

In Node.js, many asynchronous functions follow the **error-first callback pattern**, where the first argument of the callback is an error object (if an error occurs).

```javascript
fs.readFile('nonexistent-file.txt', (err, data)
=> {
    if (err) {
        console.error('Error    reading    file:',
err.message);
    } else {
        console.log(data);
    }
});
```

Here, if the file does not exist, the err argument will be populated, and you can handle it accordingly.

Debugging Tools in Node.js

Node.js comes with several built-in tools to help you debug your applications. Below are some useful debugging tools and techniques.

1. Console Logging (`console.log`)

The most basic tool for debugging in Node.js is **console logging**. It's simple, effective, and can be used throughout your code to trace values and program flow.

```javascript
const num1 = 5;
const num2 = 10;
console.log('num1:', num1, 'num2:', num2); // Debugging values
```

2. Debugger Statement

Node.js has a built-in debugger. You can use the `debugger` statement to pause your code execution and inspect variables.

```javascript
function add(a, b) {
    debugger; // This will trigger the debugger
    return a + b;
}
```

```
add(5, 3);
```

To start the Node.js debugger, run your app with the `inspect` flag:

```bash
node inspect app.js
```

This will run the program and pause at the `debugger` statement, allowing you to inspect variables and step through the code.

3. Node.js Debugging with Chrome DevTools

You can also use **Chrome DevTools** for debugging Node.js applications. To start the debugger with Chrome DevTools, run the following command:

```bash
node --inspect-brk app.js
```

This will start your Node.js app and pause execution before the first line of code. You can then open Chrome and go to `chrome://inspect` to start debugging your app.

4. Debugging with Visual Studio Code (VS Code)

VS Code has excellent built-in support for debugging Node.js applications. You can set breakpoints and inspect variables directly within the editor.

To use VS Code for debugging:

1. Open your project in VS Code.
2. Go to the **Run** panel and click on **Add Configuration**.
3. Select **Node.js: Launch Program** and configure it with the path to your app.js.
4. Set breakpoints and click the green **play** button to start debugging.

Real-World Example: Debugging an Express App

Let's walk through an example where we debug an **Express** application that has a bug. The application retrieves a list of blog posts from a database and displays them, but an error occurs when retrieving data.

Step 1: Simulate the Bug

Here's the basic structure of the Express app:

javascript

```
const express = require('express');
const app = express();
const port = 3000;

// Simulating a database call
function getPostsFromDatabase(callback) {
    setTimeout(() => {
        callback(null, [{ title: 'Post 1' }, {
title: 'Post 2' }]);
    }, 1000);
}

app.get('/posts', (req, res) => {
    getPostsFromDatabase((err, posts) => {
        if (err) {
            res.status(500).send('Error
retrieving posts');
        } else {
            res.json(posts);
        }
    });
});

app.listen(port, () => {
    console.log(`Server        running        at
http://localhost:${port}`);
});
```

Step 2: Add Debugging with `console.log`

We want to debug the data retrieval process. Let's add some `console.log()` statements:

javascript

```
app.get('/posts', (req, res) => {
    console.log('Fetching posts...'); // Log
when the request is made
    getPostsFromDatabase((err, posts) => {
        if (err) {
            console.error('Error      retrieving
posts:', err);
            res.status(500).send('Error
retrieving posts');
        } else {
            console.log('Posts      retrieved:',
posts); // Log the posts
            res.json(posts);
        }
    });
});
```

Step 3: Debugging with Breakpoints in VS Code

Set breakpoints in your code where you suspect the error might be (e.g., in the `getPostsFromDatabase` callback). Then, run the app in debug mode to inspect the variables.

Step 4: Fixing the Bug

After inspecting the logs and variables, we realize that the error occurs because the database call takes longer than expected, and the request is being made before the data is retrieved. We can fix it by improving the database handling logic (perhaps adding a proper delay or ensuring the data is available before responding).

Conclusion

In this chapter, we discussed the importance of **error handling** and **debugging** in Node.js. We covered various types of errors, how to handle synchronous and asynchronous errors using `try...catch`, promises, and callbacks. We also explored useful **debugging tools** like `console.log`, the built-in Node.js debugger, and **VS Code** for debugging. Finally, we worked through a real-world example of debugging an **Express app**.

In the next chapter, we will explore how to **optimize** your Node.js application for production by looking into performance tuning, memory management, and scaling techniques.

CHAPTER 15

TESTING NODE.JS APPLICATIONS

Testing is a critical part of building reliable and maintainable applications. In this chapter, we will discuss the importance of testing in Node.js, explore popular **testing frameworks** such as **Mocha**, **Jest**, and **Chai**, and walk through different types of testing, including **unit testing**, **integration testing**, and **mocking dependencies**. We will also build a real-world example by **unit testing a REST API** built with **Express**.

Introduction to Testing Frameworks (Mocha, Jest, Chai)

Testing frameworks are tools that help you organize and run tests in your Node.js applications. There are several testing libraries available, but the most popular ones are **Mocha**, **Jest**, and **Chai**.

Mocha

Mocha is a flexible and widely used testing framework for Node.js. It allows you to write tests in a BDD (Behavior Driven

Development) or TDD (Test Driven Development) style. Mocha supports asynchronous testing, making it well-suited for Node.js.

- **Installation**:

```bash
npm install mocha --save-dev
```

- **Basic Example**:

```javascript
const assert = require('assert');

describe('Sample Test', () => {
  it('should return true', () => {
    assert.strictEqual(true, true);
  });
});
```

Jest

Jest is a popular testing framework developed by Facebook, especially for testing React applications. It is also used in Node.js applications due to its simplicity and powerful features, such as built-in mocking, snapshot testing, and parallel test execution.

- **Installation**:

```bash
npm install jest --save-dev
```

- **Basic Example**:

```javascript
test('should return true', () => {
  expect(true).toBe(true);
});
```

Chai

Chai is an assertion library that pairs well with Mocha. It allows you to make more readable assertions in your tests and supports multiple assertion styles (e.g., BDD, TDD).

- **Installation**:

```bash
npm install chai --save-dev
```

- **Basic Example**:

```javascript
const chai = require('chai');
const expect = chai.expect;
```

```
describe('Sample Test', () => {
  it('should return true', () => {
    expect(true).to.equal(true);
  });
});
```

You can use **Mocha** or **Jest** with **Chai** for assertion functionality in your tests.

Writing Unit Tests for Node.js Code

Unit tests are designed to test a small unit of code, usually a single function or method, in isolation from the rest of the system. Unit tests help ensure that individual components work as expected.

Example: Unit Testing a Simple Function

Let's write a unit test for a simple function that adds two numbers.

1. **Create a file math.js** with the function to be tested:

```
javascript
```

```
// math.js
function add(a, b) {
    return a + b;
}
```

```
module.exports = { add };
```

2. **Create a test file math.test.js** for the unit test:

javascript

```javascript
const assert = require('assert');
const math = require('./math');

describe('add()', () => {
    it('should return 4 when adding 2 and 2', ()
=> {
        const result = math.add(2, 2);
        assert.strictEqual(result, 4);
    });

    it('should return 0 when adding -2 and 2', ()
=> {
        const result = math.add(-2, 2);
        assert.strictEqual(result, 0);
    });
});
```

3. **Run the tests** with Mocha:

bash

```bash
npx mocha math.test.js
```

This will run the tests and output the results, confirming that the add() function behaves as expected.

Mocking Dependencies

In real-world applications, functions often depend on external services, databases, or other modules. **Mocking** is a technique where you replace these external dependencies with fake objects or functions to simulate their behavior. This allows you to test the behavior of your code without relying on actual external services.

Example: Mocking a Database Call

Let's say we have a function getUser() that retrieves user data from a database.

1. **Create a file userService.js:**

javascript

```
// userService.js
const database = require('./database');

function getUser(userId) {
    return database.query(`SELECT * FROM users WHERE id = ${userId}`);
}
```

```
module.exports = { getUser };
```

2. **Mocking the `database.query()` method** using **Sinon** (a popular mocking library):
   o Install Sinon:

   ```bash
   npm install sinon --save-dev
   ```

3. **Write the unit test with mocking**:

```javascript
const sinon = require('sinon');
const assert = require('assert');
const userService = require('./userService');
const database = require('./database');

describe('getUser()', () => {
    it('should return user data', () => {
        // Mock the database.query method
        const fakeQuery = sinon.stub(database,
'query').returns({ id: 1, name: 'John Doe' });

        const user = userService.getUser(1);
        assert.deepStrictEqual(user, { id: 1,
name: 'John Doe' });
```

192

```
        fakeQuery.restore();      // Restore the
original method
    });
});
```

In this test:

- We use **Sinon** to create a fake version of the `database.query()` method.
- The test checks if the `getUser()` method correctly returns user data.

Integration Testing with Node.js

Integration tests ensure that different modules or components of your application work together correctly. Unlike unit tests, integration tests test the interaction between multiple pieces of the system, such as database calls or API endpoints.

Example: Testing an API Endpoint

Let's create an integration test for an Express API endpoint that retrieves user data.

1. **Set up the Express app** (app.js):

```
javascript
```

```javascript
const express = require('express');
const app = express();
const port = 3000;

// Mock database query function
const getUser = (userId) => {
    return { id: userId, name: 'John Doe' };
};

// Define an API route
app.get('/user/:id', (req, res) => {
    const user = getUser(req.params.id);
    res.json(user);
});

app.listen(port, () => {
    console.log(`Server          running          at
http://localhost:${port}`);
});
```

2. **Write an integration test using supertest:**

  o Install supertest for HTTP assertions:

```bash
bash
```

```bash
npm install supertest --save-dev
```

3. **Create the test file app.test.js:**

```javascript
javascript
```

194

```
const request = require('supertest');
const app = require('./app');   // Import the
Express app

describe('GET /user/:id', () => {
    it('should return user data for user ID 1',
async () => {
        const        response        =        await
request(app).get('/user/1');
        expect(response.status).toBe(200);
        expect(response.body).toEqual({ id: '1',
name: 'John Doe' });
    });
});
```

In this example:

- We use **supertest** to simulate an HTTP request to the `/user/:id` endpoint.
- The test checks that the server responds with the correct user data and a `200` status code.

Real-World Example: Unit Testing a REST API

Let's apply what we've learned by writing unit tests for a **REST API** that performs CRUD operations on a user resource.

Step 1: Set Up the API

Create a simple **Express API** with basic CRUD functionality for managing users.

1. **Create userController.js**:

javascript

```javascript
// userController.js
const users = [];

exports.createUser = (req, res) => {
    const { name, email } = req.body;
    const newUser = { id: users.length + 1, name, email };
    users.push(newUser);
    res.status(201).json(newUser);
};

exports.getUsers = (req, res) => {
    res.status(200).json(users);
};

exports.getUserById = (req, res) => {
    const user = users.find(u => u.id === parseInt(req.params.id));
    if (!user) return res.status(404).send('User not found');
```

```
    res.status(200).json(user);
};
```

2. **Create the API routes** (app.js):

javascript

```
const express = require('express');
const bodyParser = require('body-parser');
const            userController            =
require('./userController');
const app = express();

app.use(bodyParser.json());

app.post('/users', userController.createUser);
app.get('/users', userController.getUsers);
app.get('/users/:id',
userController.getUserById);

module.exports = app;
```

Step 2: Write the Unit Tests

1. **Install the necessary dependencies**:

bash

```
npm install jest supertest --save-dev
```

2. **Create app.test.js** to write the tests for the API:

197

```javascript
const request = require('supertest');
const app = require('./app');

describe('User API', () => {
    it('should create a new user', async () => {
        const response = await request(app)
            .post('/users')
            .send({ name: 'John Doe', email:
'john.doe@example.com' });

        expect(response.status).toBe(201);

expect(response.body).toHaveProperty('id');
        expect(response.body.name).toBe('John
Doe');
    });

    it('should fetch all users', async () => {
        const         response         =         await
request(app).get('/users');
        expect(response.status).toBe(200);

expect(Array.isArray(response.body)).toBe(true)
;
    });
```

```
    it('should fetch a user by ID', async () =>
{
        const          response         =          await
request(app).get('/users/1');
        expect(response.status).toBe(200);
        expect(response.body.name).toBe('John
Doe');
    });

    it('should return 404 if user not found',
async () => {
        const          response         =          await
request(app).get('/users/999');
        expect(response.status).toBe(404);
    });
});
```

Step 3: Run the Tests

To run the tests, use **Jest**:

```bash
bash
```

```
npx jest app.test.js
```

Conclusion

In this chapter, we learned about **testing** in Node.js, focusing on popular testing frameworks like **Mocha**, **Jest**, and **Chai**. We

199

covered how to write **unit tests** for Node.js code, how to **mock dependencies**, and how to perform **integration testing**. Finally, we walked through a real-world example of **unit testing a REST API** built with **Express**.

Testing is crucial for ensuring the reliability and correctness of your code. In the next chapter, we will explore **performance optimization** techniques in Node.js to ensure your application runs efficiently at scale.

CHAPTER 16

NODE.JS PERFORMANCE AND OPTIMIZATION

Performance and scalability are crucial factors for building efficient and high-performing web applications. In this chapter, we will cover the key concepts of **Node.js performance**, how to profile and monitor your applications, techniques to **optimize Node.js applications**, and best practices for **scaling**. We'll also walk through a **real-world example** of improving the performance of a web app.

Understanding Node.js Performance Issues

Node.js is known for its non-blocking, event-driven architecture, but certain performance issues can still arise due to the nature of asynchronous programming and the single-threaded event loop. Here are some common performance bottlenecks:

1. Blocking Code

Although Node.js is non-blocking, if you have blocking operations, such as synchronous I/O (e.g., `fs.readFileSync()`), it can prevent the event loop from processing other requests, leading to performance degradation.

2. Heavy CPU-bound Operations

Node.js is single-threaded, meaning it can only process one operation at a time. If there is a CPU-bound task like heavy computation or complex algorithms running synchronously, it can block the event loop and cause delays in processing other requests.

3. Memory Leaks

Memory leaks in Node.js can cause your application to gradually consume more memory, slowing down performance and eventually causing crashes or application downtime.

4. Inefficient Database Queries

Poorly optimized database queries can become a performance bottleneck. It's essential to optimize database access by using proper indexing, pagination, and caching strategies.

5. Unoptimized Dependencies

Using inefficient or heavy dependencies can reduce the overall performance of your Node.js app. Always keep an eye on the performance impact of third-party modules.

Profiling and Monitoring Node.js Apps

1. Profiling Node.js Applications

Profiling helps you measure the performance of your application by identifying bottlenecks and hotspots. Here are a few ways to profile a Node.js app:

Node.js Built-in Profiler

Node.js comes with a built-in profiler that you can use to analyze CPU usage and performance. You can run your app in profiling mode by using the following command:

```bash
```

```bash
node --inspect-brk app.js
```

This will start the app and open a debugging session in Chrome DevTools. You can open `chrome://inspect` in Google Chrome to start debugging and profiling.

Using `node --prof`

To generate a detailed profile of your application, you can use the `--prof` flag:

```bash
```

```
node --prof app.js
```

This will output profiling information to a file, which can be analyzed for performance bottlenecks.

2. Monitoring Node.js Applications

For real-time monitoring of your Node.js app, consider using tools such as **PM2**, **New Relic**, or **Datadog**.

PM2

PM2 is a popular process manager for Node.js applications that provides monitoring, clustering, and performance management features. It helps monitor the CPU and memory usage of your application in real-time.

Install PM2 globally:

```bash
npm install pm2 -g
```

Start your app with PM2:

```bash
pm2 start app.js
```

To monitor the app:

```bash
bash
```

```bash
pm2 monit
```

PM2 provides metrics on CPU usage, memory consumption, and request rates.

New Relic

New Relic is a powerful application performance monitoring tool that provides detailed insights into your Node.js app's performance, including slow transactions, error rates, and resource consumption.

To integrate New Relic into your app:

1. Sign up for New Relic and get your license key.
2. Install the New Relic package:

```bash
bash
```

```bash
npm install newrelic --save
```

3. Add the following code at the very top of your `app.js`:

```javascript
javascript
```

```javascript
require('newrelic');
```

New Relic will start monitoring your app and provide detailed insights on your dashboard.

Optimizing Node.js Applications

1. Avoid Blocking Operations

Ensure that you avoid **blocking operations** like `fs.readFileSync()`, `child_process.execSync()`, or synchronous database queries. Always use asynchronous methods to ensure non-blocking behavior and keep the event loop free.

Example:

```javascript
// Synchronous (blocks event loop)
const fs = require('fs');
const data = fs.readFileSync('largeFile.txt');

// Asynchronous (non-blocking)
fs.readFile('largeFile.txt', 'utf8', (err, data)
=> {
    if (err) {
        console.error('Error    reading    file:',
err);
    } else {
        console.log(data);
    }
```

```
});
```

2. Offload CPU-intensive Work

Since Node.js runs on a single thread, heavy CPU-bound tasks (like image processing, encryption, or complex calculations) should be offloaded to separate processes or worker threads. You can use the **worker_threads** module or external services to offload these tasks.

Example of using **worker_threads**:

javascript

```
const { Worker, isMainThread, parentPort } =
require('worker_threads');

if (isMainThread) {
    // Main thread: Spawn a worker
    const worker = new Worker(__filename);
    worker.on('message',        (msg)        =>
console.log(msg));
    worker.postMessage('Start CPU-bound task');
} else {
    // Worker thread: Perform CPU-intensive task
    parentPort.on('message', (message) => {
        if (message === 'Start CPU-bound task')
{
            // Simulate a CPU-intensive task
```

```
        const          result          =
performComplexComputation();
        parentPort.postMessage(result);
    }
  });


  function performComplexComputation() {
    // Simulated CPU-intensive task
    return 'Computation complete';
  }
}
```

3. Efficient Database Access

Ensure that your database queries are efficient by:

- Using **indexes** to speed up queries.
- **Batching** requests to reduce the number of calls.
- Implementing **pagination** for large datasets.

Example of adding an index to a MongoDB query:

```javascript

// Create an index on the 'username' field
User.createIndex({ username: 1 });
```

4. Caching

Caching can significantly improve the performance of your app by reducing the number of times you query the database or external services.

- Use in-memory caching with **Redis** or **Memcached** to cache frequently requested data.
- Cache HTTP responses using **HTTP cache headers** or reverse proxies like **Varnish**.

Example of using **Redis** for caching:

javascript

```javascript
const redis = require('redis');
const client = redis.createClient();

function getUserData(userId) {
    client.get(userId, (err, data) => {
        if (data) {
            console.log('Cache hit');
            return JSON.parse(data);
        } else {
            console.log('Cache miss');
            // Fetch data from the database
            const                user               =
fetchUserFromDatabase(userId);
```

```
        client.setex(userId,              3600,
JSON.stringify(user));  // Cache for 1 hour
        return user;
    }
  });
}
```

Best Practices for Scaling Node.js Apps

When your Node.js app grows, you need to ensure it can handle increased traffic and scale effectively.

1. Use Cluster Module for Horizontal Scaling

Node.js runs on a single thread, but you can use the **cluster module** to take advantage of multiple CPU cores. This allows you to run multiple instances of your app across different cores.

Example:

javascript

```
const cluster = require('cluster');
const http = require('http');
const os = require('os');

if (cluster.isMaster) {
    const numCPUs = os.cpus().length;
    for (let i = 0; i < numCPUs; i++) {
```

210

```
      cluster.fork();
   }

   cluster.on('exit', (worker, code, signal) =>
{
      console.log(`Worker
${worker.process.pid} died`);
   });
} else {
   http.createServer((req, res) => {
      res.writeHead(200);
      res.end('Hello, world!');
   }).listen(8000);
}
```

2. Load Balancing

For production environments, use **load balancers** (such as **NGINX** or **AWS Elastic Load Balancing**) to distribute incoming traffic across multiple instances of your app, ensuring high availability and fault tolerance.

3. Implement Graceful Shutdown

Implementing **graceful shutdown** ensures that when your app is restarted or terminated, it closes connections and completes any ongoing requests without dropping them.

```
javascript
```

```
process.on('SIGTERM', () => {
    server.close(() => {
        console.log('Server      gracefully      shut
down');
    });
});
```

Real-World Example: Improving Performance of a Web App

Let's say we have a simple **Express web app** that serves user data and a list of posts. We notice performance degradation as the app scales.

Initial Issues:

- Blocking database queries that slow down response times.
- No caching, causing repetitive database calls.
- Slow responses due to heavy CPU-bound calculations.

Optimizations:

- Replace **blocking database queries** with asynchronous calls.
- Implement **Redis caching** for user data and posts.
- Offload heavy CPU-bound work to **worker threads**.

Optimized Code Example:

1. Async Database Queries:

javascript

```javascript
// Use async/await with MongoDB to fetch user data
async function getUserData(userId) {
    return await User.findById(userId).exec();
}
```

2. Caching User Data with Redis:

javascript

```javascript
const redis = require('redis');
const client = redis.createClient();

async function getUserDataWithCache(userId) {
    return new Promise((resolve, reject) => {
        client.get(userId, async (err, cachedData) => {
            if (cachedData) {
                return resolve(JSON.parse(cachedData));
            } else {
                const user = await getUserData(userId);
```

```
        client.setex(userId,        3600,
JSON.stringify(user));  // Cache for 1 hour
        return resolve(user);
    }
  });
});
}
```

Conclusion

In this chapter, we covered **Node.js performance** and **optimization** techniques, focusing on profiling and monitoring your applications, optimizing code for speed, and using best practices for scaling. We learned how to avoid blocking operations, offload CPU-bound tasks, use caching, and implement horizontal scaling using the cluster module. The real-world example demonstrated how to improve the performance of a web app by optimizing database queries, using caching, and offloading heavy computation.

In the next chapter, we will explore **deploying Node.js applications** to production environments, including deployment strategies, continuous integration, and monitoring in production.

CHAPTER 17

WORKING WITH FILE SYSTEMS IN NODE.JS

Node.js provides powerful tools for interacting with the **file system** (FS) on the server. Whether you need to read or write files, handle streams for large file transfers, or manage file uploads and downloads, Node.js makes these tasks straightforward and efficient. In this chapter, we will explore how to work with the file system in Node.js, focusing on **reading and writing files**, **working with streams**, and **handling file uploads and downloads**. We'll conclude with a **real-world example** of building a **file upload feature**.

Reading and Writing Files in Node.js

Node.js provides both **synchronous** and **asynchronous** methods for reading and writing files. The asynchronous methods are typically preferred in production applications, as they prevent blocking the event loop.

1. Synchronous File Operations

These operations block the event loop, meaning that the program will wait until the file is fully read or written before continuing execution.

- **Reading a file synchronously**:

```javascript
const fs = require('fs');

try {
  const data = fs.readFileSync('file.txt', 'utf8');
  console.log('File data:', data);
} catch (err) {
  console.error('Error  reading  file:', err);
}
```

- **Writing to a file synchronously**:

```javascript
const fs = require('fs');

try {
  fs.writeFileSync('output.txt',  'Hello, world!', 'utf8');
```

216

```
    console.log('File                written
successfully');
} catch (err) {
    console.error('Error   writing   file:',
err);
}
```

2. Asynchronous File Operations

Asynchronous methods allow the Node.js event loop to continue processing other tasks while file operations are in progress.

- **Reading a file asynchronously**:

```javascript

const fs = require('fs');

fs.readFile('file.txt',    'utf8',    (err,
data) => {
  if (err) {
    console.error('Error   reading   file:',
err);
  } else {
    console.log('File data:', data);
  }
});
```

- **Writing to a file asynchronously**:

```javascript
```

```
const fs = require('fs');

fs.writeFile('output.txt',          'Hello,
world!', 'utf8', (err) => {
  if (err) {
    console.error('Error  writing  file:',
err);
  } else {
    console.log('File                written
successfully');
  }
});
```

Choosing Between Synchronous and Asynchronous

- Use **synchronous methods** for small, one-time file operations that do not affect the performance of the application (e.g., configuration files or scripts).
- Use **asynchronous methods** for reading or writing large files or performing operations in production environments where you need to avoid blocking the event loop.

Working with Streams in Node.js

Streams in Node.js are a powerful way to handle large amounts of data. Instead of loading an entire file into memory, streams

218

allow you to process data in chunks, which is more memory-efficient.

1. Readable Streams

Readable streams allow you to read data from a source (e.g., a file, HTTP response, or database) in chunks.

- **Example: Reading a file using streams**:

```javascript
const fs = require('fs');
const readableStream = fs.createReadStream('largeFile.txt', 'utf8');

readableStream.on('data', (chunk) => {
  console.log('Received chunk:', chunk);
});

readableStream.on('end', () => {
  console.log('File reading complete');
});

readableStream.on('error', (err) => {
  console.error('Error reading file:', err);
});
```

In this example:

- The **data** event is triggered whenever a chunk of data is read from the file.
- The **end** event is triggered when the entire file has been read.
- The **error** event handles any read errors.

2. Writable Streams

Writable streams allow you to write data to a destination (e.g., a file, database, or HTTP response).

- **Example: Writing data to a file using streams**:

```javascript
const fs = require('fs');
const            writableStream            =
fs.createWriteStream('output.txt',
'utf8');

writableStream.write('Hello, world!\n');
writableStream.write('Node.js streams are
awesome!\n');

writableStream.end(() => {
  console.log('Writing complete');
});
```

```
writableStream.on('error', (err) => {
  console.error('Error writing to file:',
err);
});
```

In this example:

- We use **write()** to write data in chunks.
- The **end()** method signals that no more data will be written.

3. Piping Streams

You can **pipe** readable streams to writable streams, allowing you to transfer data from one stream to another without loading it entirely into memory.

- **Example: Piping data from a file to another file**:

```javascript
const fs = require('fs');
const          readableStream          =
fs.createReadStream('largeFile.txt');
const          writableStream          =
fs.createWriteStream('OfFile.txt');

readableStream.pipe(writableStream);
```

```
writableStream.on('finish', () => {
  console.log('File copied successfully');
});


writableStream.on('error', (err) => {
  console.error('Error   during   file   :',
err);
});
```

This method is especially useful when dealing with large files, as it avoids reading the entire file into memory at once.

Handling File Uploads and Downloads

Handling **file uploads** and **downloads** is common in many web applications, and Node.js provides several modules to make it easier to handle these tasks.

1. Handling File Uploads

The most common approach to handling file uploads in Node.js is by using the **Multer** middleware for **Express**. Multer handles multipart form-data, which is used for uploading files.

- **Install Multer**:

bash

```
npm install multer --save
```

- **Example: File upload with Multer**:

```javascript
const express = require('express');
const multer = require('multer');
const path = require('path');

const app = express();
const upload = multer({ dest: 'uploads/' });

app.post('/upload', upload.single('file'),
(req, res) => {
  console.log('Uploaded file:', req.file);
  res.send('File uploaded successfully');
});

app.listen(3000, () => {
  console.log('Server       running       on
http://localhost:3000');
});
```

In this example:

- **upload.single('file')** tells Multer to handle a single file upload with the field name file.

223

- The uploaded file is saved to the `uploads/` directory.

2. Handling File Downloads

You can serve files directly to clients by using the `res.download()` method in Express.

- **Example: File download**:

```javascript
const express = require('express');
const app = express();

app.get('/download', (req, res) => {
  const filePath = 'uploads/sampleFile.txt';
  res.download(filePath, 'downloadedFile.txt', (err) => {
    if (err) {
      console.error('Error downloading file:', err);
    }
  });
});

app.listen(3000, () => {
  console.log('Server running on http://localhost:3000');
```

224

```
});
```

In this example:

- **res.download(filePath)** prompts the client to download the file located at filePath.
- The second argument specifies the filename to be used for the downloaded file.

Real-World Example: Building a File Upload Feature

Let's build a **file upload feature** for an Express app where users can upload an image and store it on the server.

Step 1: Install Dependencies

Install **Express** and **Multer**:

```bash
```

```
npm install express multer --save
```

Step 2: Set Up the Server

Create a file app.js:

```javascript
```

```
const express = require('express');
```

```
const multer = require('multer');
const path = require('path');

const app = express();

// Configure Multer storage settings
const storage = multer.diskStorage({
  destination: (req, file, cb) => {
    cb(null, 'uploads/');
  },
  filename: (req, file, cb) => {
    cb(null,            Date.now()            +
path.extname(file.originalname));
  }
});

const upload = multer({ storage: storage });

// Serve static files from the 'uploads'
directory
app.use('/uploads', express.static('uploads'));

// Handle file upload
app.post('/upload',      upload.single('image'),
(req, res) => {
  if (!req.file) {
    return    res.status(400).send('No      file
uploaded');
  }
```

```
res.send(`File    uploaded    successfully:    <a
href="/uploads/${req.file.filename}">View
file</a>`);
});


app.listen(3000, () => {
  console.log('Server           running           at
http://localhost:3000');
});
```

Step 3: Testing the Upload

1. Start the server:

```bash

node app.js
```

2. Use **Postman** or an HTML form to upload an image:
   - o URL: http://localhost:3000/upload
   - o Method: POST
   - o Field   Name: image   (same   as
     upload.single('image') in the code)

3. After uploading, the server responds with a link to view the uploaded image.

227

Conclusion

In this chapter, we covered how to interact with the **file system** in Node.js. We explored how to read and write files synchronously and asynchronously, how to work with **streams** to efficiently handle large files, and how to implement **file uploads** and **downloads** in a web app. We also built a **real-world example** of a file upload feature using **Multer**.

Understanding how to work with files is essential for many applications, and by following the techniques and best practices in this chapter, you can efficiently handle file operations in your Node.js applications.

In the next chapter, we will look into **security** best practices in Node.js to ensure your applications are safe from common vulnerabilities.

CHAPTER 18

CACHING IN NODE.JS

Caching is one of the most effective techniques to improve the performance of web applications by reducing the time spent fetching data from databases or external APIs. In this chapter, we will discuss the concept of **caching** in Node.js, explore **memory caching with Redis**, and learn how to **cache responses** in web applications. We'll also walk through a **real-world example** of caching **API responses** to improve performance.

What is Caching?

Caching is the process of storing frequently accessed data in a temporary storage location (cache) to reduce the time it takes to retrieve the data when needed again. Instead of fetching the same data from the source (e.g., database or external API) each time, the system retrieves it from the cache, which is much faster.

Types of Caching:

1. **Memory Caching**: Storing data in memory (RAM) for quick retrieval. This is typically done using in-memory data stores like **Redis** or **Memcached**.

229

2. **Database Caching**: Caching query results or frequently requested data in the database itself to avoid repeated queries.

3. **File Caching**: Storing file data (such as images or documents) in a cache for faster access.

4. **HTTP Caching**: Caching responses from web servers to reduce the load on the server and improve client-side performance (e.g., **browser cache**, **CDN cache**).

Why Use Caching?

- **Reduced Latency**: Accessing data from the cache is much faster than querying a database or making API calls.

- **Lower Load on Databases/External Services**: By caching frequently requested data, the pressure on your database or external services is reduced, leading to better scalability.

- **Improved User Experience**: Faster response times mean a smoother and more responsive user experience.

Memory Caching with Redis

Redis is an in-memory key-value store that is often used as a cache to speed up web applications. Redis is highly performant and supports complex data types such as strings, hashes, lists, sets, and sorted sets.

230

Installing Redis

1. **Install Redis**:
   - On Linux, you can install Redis using your package manager:

     bash

     ```
     sudo apt-get install redis-server
     ```

   - On macOS, you can use **Homebrew**:

     bash

     ```
     brew install redis
     ```

2. **Start Redis**: After installation, start Redis with:

   bash

   ```
   redis-server
   ```

3. **Install Redis Client for Node.js**: Use the **redis** package to interact with Redis in your Node.js application.

   bash

   ```
   npm install redis --save
   ```

231

Basic Redis Usage in Node.js

1. **Connecting to Redis**:

```javascript
const redis = require('redis');
const client = redis.createClient();   //
Default connection on localhost:6379

client.on('connect', () => {
    console.log('Connected to Redis');
});
```

2. **Setting and Getting Cache Data**: Redis allows you to store data as key-value pairs. The basic operations are set() and get().

   o **Setting Data**:

   ```javascript
   client.set('name',     'John     Doe',
   redis.print);   // Store 'John Doe'
   with key 'name'
   ```

   o **Getting Data**:

   ```javascript
   client.get('name', (err, reply) => {
   ```

232

```
    if (err) throw err;
    console.log(reply);   // Output:
John Doe
});
```

3. **Caching Expiry Time**: Redis allows you to set an expiry time for cache data using the EX parameter in the set() method.

```javascript

client.setex('name', 3600, 'John Doe');   //
Expiry time of 1 hour (3600 seconds)
```

Caching Responses in Web Applications

In web applications, caching is commonly used to store HTTP responses. By caching responses, you can reduce the load on your server and improve response times for users. One common use case is caching API responses.

1. Caching API Responses

API responses are ideal candidates for caching, especially for data that doesn't change frequently. By caching the responses, you can serve subsequent requests faster and reduce the load on your database or third-party APIs.

Example: Caching API Responses Using Redis

Let's create a simple **Express API** and cache the responses for performance improvement.

1. **Setting Up the Express Server**: Install the required dependencies:

bash

```
npm install express redis --save
```

Create the file app.js:

javascript

```
const express = require('express');
const redis = require('redis');
const app = express();
const client = redis.createClient();

// Sample API endpoint that fetches data
app.get('/data', (req, res) => {
    const cacheKey = 'userData';

    // Check if data is in cache
    client.get(cacheKey, (err, cachedData)
=> {
        if (err) throw err;
```

```
        if (cachedData) {
            console.log('Cache hit');
            return
res.json(JSON.parse(cachedData));        //
Return cached data
        }

        console.log('Cache miss');
        // Simulate database or external
API call
        const data = { name: 'John Doe',
age: 30, location: 'USA' };

        // Store the data in cache for
future requests (with 1 hour expiration)
        client.setex(cacheKey,       3600,
JSON.stringify(data));

        return res.json(data);   // Return
fresh data
    });
});

app.listen(3000, () => {
    console.log('Server     running     at
http://localhost:3000');
});
```

2. **How It Works**:

○ When a client makes a request to /data, the server first checks if the response is cached in Redis.

○ If the cache contains the data (a cache hit), the server sends the cached response to the client.

○ If the cache is empty (a cache miss), the server generates the response, stores it in the cache for subsequent requests, and sends it to the client.

3. **Test the Cache**: Start the server:

```bash
```

```
node app.js
```

Visit http://localhost:3000/data in your browser or use **Postman**. On the first request, you will see a "Cache miss", and subsequent requests will return the cached response with a "Cache hit".

Real-World Example: Caching API Responses for Performance

Let's enhance the previous example by adding a dynamic endpoint that retrieves user data from a database (or a mock database), with caching to speed up repeated requests.

1. **Simulate Database Query**: Suppose we have an API that fetches a list of users from a database. In this case, we will simulate the database query.

    javascript

    ```javascript
    const usersDatabase = [
        { id: 1, name: 'Alice', age: 25 },
        { id: 2, name: 'Bob', age: 30 },
        { id: 3, name: 'Charlie', age: 35 },
    ];

    // Simulate a database query
    function getUserFromDatabase(userId) {
        return    usersDatabase.find(user    =>
    user.id === userId);
    }
    ```

2. **Cache the User Data**: Modify the /user/:id endpoint to cache the user data:

    javascript

    ```javascript
    app.get('/user/:id', (req, res) => {
        const userId = req.params.id;
        const cacheKey = `user:${userId}`;

        // Check if data is in the cache
    ```

```
client.get(cacheKey, (err, cachedData)
=> {
        if (err) throw err;

        if (cachedData) {
            console.log('Cache hit');
            return
res.json(JSON.parse(cachedData));        //
Return cached data
        }

        console.log('Cache miss');
        // Simulate a database query to
fetch user data
        const          user          =
getUserFromDatabase(Number(userId));

        if (!user) {
            return
res.status(404).send('User not found');
        }

        // Store the user data in cache for
future requests (with 1 hour expiration)
        client.setex(cacheKey,        3600,
JSON.stringify(user));

        return res.json(user);   // Return
user data
```

```
  });
});
```

3. **Test the Cache with Dynamic Data**:
   - When you visit `http://localhost:3000/user/1` for the first time, the server will simulate a database query, store the data in the cache, and return the response.
   - Subsequent requests to the same endpoint will fetch the data from the cache, significantly reducing response time.

Conclusion

In this chapter, we explored the importance of **caching** in Node.js applications and discussed how to implement **memory caching with Redis** to speed up your application. We also covered techniques for **caching API responses** to improve performance and reduce the load on databases or external services. By using Redis for caching, you can ensure that frequently accessed data is served quickly, leading to faster response times and better scalability.

In the next chapter, we will explore **security best practices** in Node.js to protect your application from common vulnerabilities.

CHAPTER 19

DEPLOYING NODE.JS APPLICATIONS

Once your Node.js application is ready for production, the next step is deployment. In this chapter, we will discuss various deployment options for Node.js applications, including hosting on platforms like **Heroku, AWS**, and **DigitalOcean**. We will also cover the importance of **Continuous Integration and Continuous Deployment (CI/CD)** and walk through a **real-world example** of deploying an **Express app** to production.

Hosting Node.js Apps on Heroku

Heroku is a popular cloud platform that allows you to quickly deploy, manage, and scale applications. Heroku abstracts away the infrastructure and provides an easy-to-use interface for deploying Node.js applications.

Step 1: Setting Up Your Application for Heroku

Before deploying to Heroku, make sure your Node.js application is ready:

1. Your app must have a **package.json** file that defines the dependencies.

2. You should define a **start script** in the package.json file to tell Heroku how to start your application.

```json
{
  "scripts": {
    "start": "node app.js"
  }
}
```

Step 2: Install the Heroku CLI

To deploy your app to Heroku, you need the **Heroku Command Line Interface (CLI)**:

1. Download and install the Heroku CLI from Heroku's website.

2. Once installed, log in to your Heroku account by running:

```bash
heroku login
```

241

Step 3: Deploying Your Application

1. **Initialize a Git Repository**: Ensure your project is version-controlled with **Git**. If your project is not already a Git repository, initialize it:

   bash

   ```
   git init
   git add .
   git commit -m "Initial commit"
   ```

2. **Create a Heroku App**: Run the following command to create a new app on Heroku:

   bash

   ```
   heroku create
   ```

   This command will automatically create a new app and associate it with your Git repository.

3. **Deploy the App to Heroku**: Push your app to Heroku using Git:

   bash

   ```
   git push heroku master
   ```

4. **Access Your App**: Once the deployment is complete, Heroku will provide a URL where your application is hosted:

bash

```
heroku open
```

5. **Scaling Your App**: Heroku uses **dynos** (lightweight containers) to run your app. To scale your app, you can add more dynos:

bash

```
heroku ps:scale web=1
```

Setting Up Node.js with AWS or DigitalOcean

For more control over your application and infrastructure, you can host your Node.js application on **AWS (Amazon Web Services)** or **DigitalOcean**.

1. Hosting on AWS (EC2)

AWS offers a wide range of services, but **EC2 (Elastic Compute Cloud)** is typically used to host Node.js applications.

Step 1: Launch an EC2 Instance

1. Go to the AWS Management Console and launch a new EC2 instance (choose **Ubuntu** as the operating system).
2. Choose a key pair for SSH access to the instance.

Step 2: Connect to the EC2 Instance

Once the EC2 instance is running, you can connect to it using SSH:

bash

```
ssh -i "your-key-pair.pem" ubuntu@your-ec2-public-ip
```

Step 3: Install Node.js and Dependencies

Once connected to the instance, install Node.js:

bash

```
sudo apt update
sudo apt install nodejs
sudo apt install npm
```

Clone your Node.js application from Git:

bash

```
git                                    clone
https://github.com/yourusername/yourapp.git
cd yourapp
```

Install the app dependencies:

```
bash
```

```
npm install
```

Step 4: Start Your Application

You can start your Node.js app using **PM2** (a process manager for Node.js):

```
bash
```

```
npm install pm2 -g
pm2 start app.js
```

PM2 ensures that your app runs continuously and can be restarted automatically in case of crashes.

Step 5: Open the Required Ports

Make sure the **EC2 Security Group** is configured to allow HTTP traffic (port 80) and any other ports your app uses.

2. Hosting on DigitalOcean

DigitalOcean provides cloud computing services and is known for its simplicity and developer-friendly interface.

Step 1: Create a Droplet

1. Go to the **DigitalOcean** dashboard and create a new **Droplet** (a virtual server).
2. Choose an image (e.g., Ubuntu).
3. Select the plan and data center region.

Step 2: Connect to the Droplet

Once the Droplet is created, connect to it using SSH:

bash

```
ssh root@your-droplet-ip
```

Step 3: Install Node.js and Your Application

Install Node.js, Git, and other dependencies just like with AWS:

bash

```
sudo apt update
sudo apt install nodejs npm git
```

Clone your application and install dependencies:

```
bash
```

```
git                                    clone
https://github.com/yourusername/yourapp.git
cd yourapp
npm install
```

Start the app using **PM2** to ensure it runs continuously:

```
bash
```

```
npm install pm2 -g
pm2 start app.js
```

Continuous Deployment with CI/CD

Continuous Integration (CI) and **Continuous Deployment (CD)** are practices that automate the process of integrating code changes and deploying them to production environments. This leads to more reliable releases and faster development cycles.

1. Setting Up CI/CD with GitHub Actions

GitHub Actions is a popular CI/CD tool that integrates directly with GitHub repositories. It allows you to automate tasks like running tests, building, and deploying your Node.js application.

Step 1: Create a GitHub Action Workflow

1. In your project's GitHub repository, create a `.github/workflows` directory.

2. Create a YAML file (`ci-cd.yml`) in this directory to define the workflow:

```yaml
yaml

name: CI/CD Pipeline

on:
  push:
    branches:
      - master

jobs:
  build:
    runs-on: ubuntu-latest

    steps:
      - name: Checkout code
        uses: actions/checkout@v2

      - name: Set up Node.js
        uses: actions/setup-node@v2
        with:
          node-version: '14'
```

```
- name: Install dependencies
  run: npm install


- name: Run tests
  run: npm test


- name: Deploy to Heroku
  uses:          akshnz/heroku-deploy-
action@v1.0.1
  with:
    heroku_api_key:             ${{
secrets.HEROKU_API_KEY }}
    heroku_app_name:    your-heroku-
app-name
    heroku_email:               ${{
secrets.HEROKU_EMAIL }}
```

Step 2: Set Up Secrets

You will need to store your **Heroku API key** and **Heroku email** as **GitHub Secrets** to securely authenticate with Heroku.

1. Go to the **GitHub repository settings**.
2. Click **Secrets** on the left sidebar and add the following secrets:
   o **HEROKU_API_KEY**: Your Heroku API key.
   o **HEROKU_EMAIL**: Your Heroku account email.

Step 3: Deploy Automatically

Whenever you push code to the **master** branch, GitHub Actions will automatically:

1. Install dependencies.
2. Run tests.
3. Deploy your app to **Heroku**.

2. Using CircleCI for CI/CD

You can also use **CircleCI**, a popular CI/CD platform. It integrates with GitHub repositories to automate testing and deployment.

Real-World Example: Deploying an Express App to Production

Let's deploy a simple **Express app** to **Heroku** using the steps we've learned.

1. **Create an Express App**: First, ensure you have an Express app with a `package.json` file, like the following:

bash

```
mkdir myapp
cd myapp
```

```
npm init -y
npm install express
```

Create an `app.js` file:

```javascript
const express = require('express');
const app = express();

app.get('/', (req, res) => {
  res.send('Hello, world!');
});

app.listen(process.env.PORT || 3000, () =>
{
  console.log('Server is running...');
});
```

2. **Initialize a Git Repository**: Initialize Git in the project directory and make your first commit:

```bash
git init
git add .
git commit -m "Initial commit"
```

3. **Create a Heroku App**: Login to Heroku via the CLI and create an app:

```bash
bash
```

```bash
heroku login
heroku create
```

4. **Deploy to Heroku**: Push your code to Heroku's Git repository:

```bash
bash
```

```bash
git push heroku master
```

5. **Access Your Application**: After deployment, you can open your app in the browser with:

```bash
bash
```

```bash
heroku open
```

Your Express app is now live on Heroku!

Conclusion

In this chapter, we learned how to deploy **Node.js applications** to various hosting platforms, including **Heroku**, **AWS EC2**, and **DigitalOcean**. We also explored **Continuous Integration/Continuous Deployment (CI/CD)** to automate the process of testing and deploying your applications. We walked through a real-world example of deploying a simple **Express app** to production on Heroku.

In the next chapter, we will focus on **security best practices** for Node.js applications to ensure they are protected from common vulnerabilities.

CHAPTER 20

SECURITY BEST PRACTICES FOR NODE.JS

Security is a crucial aspect of any application, and Node.js is no exception. In this chapter, we will explore common web security vulnerabilities, best practices for securing **Express** applications, how to implement **HTTPS** and **SSL/TLS**, the importance of **security headers**, and how to prevent attacks like **Cross-Site Scripting (XSS)**. We'll wrap up with a **real-world example** of hardening an **API** against common attacks.

Understanding Common Web Security Vulnerabilities

The web is full of security threats, and Node.js applications can be vulnerable to many of these if not properly secured. Here are some of the most common security vulnerabilities:

1. SQL Injection

SQL Injection occurs when an attacker is able to manipulate SQL queries by injecting malicious code into input fields. This can lead to unauthorized data access, modification, or even deletion.

254

How to prevent it:

- Use **parameterized queries** or **ORMs (Object-Relational Mappers)** that automatically escape user input.
- Example using **prepared statements** with a SQL library:

```javascript
const db = require('pg'); // PostgreSQL example

const query = 'SELECT * FROM users WHERE id = $1';
const values = [userId];

db.query(query, values, (err, res) => {
    if (err) {
        console.error(err);
    } else {
        console.log(res.rows);
    }
});
```

2. Cross-Site Scripting (XSS)

XSS occurs when an attacker injects malicious JavaScript code into a webpage, which can execute in the browser of another user. This can lead to session hijacking, defacement, or theft of sensitive data.

255

How to prevent it:

- Always **escape user input** before rendering it on the page.
- Use libraries like **DOMPurify** or **Express-Helmet** to sanitize input.
- Avoid using `innerHTML` to inject content into your webpage.

3. Cross-Site Request Forgery (CSRF)

CSRF exploits the trust a site has in a user's browser. It tricks the user into submitting a request on their behalf (e.g., changing their email, password, etc.) without their knowledge.

How to prevent it:

- Use **anti-CSRF tokens** for sensitive requests.
- Example using **csurf** middleware in Express:

```javascript
const csrf = require('csurf');
const csrfProtection = csrf({ cookie: true
});

app.use(csrfProtection);

app.get('/form', (req, res) => {
```

```
res.render('form',        {        csrfToken:
req.csrfToken() });
});
```

4. Insecure Deserialization

Insecure deserialization occurs when an attacker manipulates serialized data (e.g., JSON or XML) that the server deserializes, leading to the execution of arbitrary code or bypassing authorization mechanisms.

How to prevent it:

- Never deserialize data from untrusted sources.
- Use **JWT** (JSON Web Tokens) for secure and stateless user sessions.

5. Security Misconfiguration

Security misconfiguration happens when a server or app is improperly configured, leaving it open to attacks. For example, exposing unnecessary services, debug information, or insecure default configurations.

How to prevent it:

- Regularly audit and review your application's configuration.

- Disable unnecessary services, ports, and debug information.

Securing Express Applications

Express is a popular framework for building web applications with Node.js. It provides many built-in features that help secure applications, but there are additional steps you need to take to make sure your application is properly secured.

1. Use Helmet to Set Security Headers

Helmet is a middleware for Express that helps secure your app by setting various HTTP headers, such as those for preventing XSS, clickjacking, and more.

- Install Helmet:

```bash
npm install helmet --save
```

- Use Helmet in your app:

```javascript
const express = require('express');
const helmet = require('helmet');
```

```
const app = express();

// Use helmet to secure HTTP headers
app.use(helmet());
```

Helmet includes several security features, such as:

- **Content-Security-Policy (CSP)**: Helps prevent XSS by specifying which resources are allowed.
- **X-Content-Type-Options**: Prevents browsers from interpreting files as something else (e.g., JavaScript as CSS).
- **Strict-Transport-Security (HSTS)**: Forces the use of HTTPS for all requests.

2. Preventing Cross-Site Scripting (XSS)

XSS attacks can be mitigated by:

- **Escaping dynamic content**: Always escape user input before inserting it into the DOM.
- **Sanitizing user input**: Use libraries like **DOMPurify** to clean HTML input before rendering.

Example:

```javascript
const DOMPurify = require('dompurify');
```

```
const express = require('express');
const app = express();

app.get('/user/:username', (req, res) => {
  const username = req.params.username;
  const            safeUsername            =
DOMPurify.sanitize(username);
  res.send(`Hello, ${safeUsername}`);
});
```

Using HTTPS and SSL/TLS

SSL/TLS encrypts data between the server and the client, ensuring secure communication. **HTTPS** is the secure version of HTTP, utilizing SSL/TLS for encryption.

1. Setting Up HTTPS

For production, it is essential to use **HTTPS** to ensure the security of data in transit.

Step 1: Generate an SSL Certificate

For development, you can generate a self-signed certificate, but for production, you should get a certificate from a trusted certificate authority (CA) like **Let's Encrypt** or **DigiCert**.

To generate a self-signed certificate:

bash

```
openssl req -nodes -new -x509 -keyout server.key
-out server.cert
```

Step 2: Enabling HTTPS in Express

To enable HTTPS, you need to use the `https` module and provide the certificate and key files:

javascript

```
const fs = require('fs');
const https = require('https');
const express = require('express');
const app = express();

const options = {
  key: fs.readFileSync('server.key'),
  cert: fs.readFileSync('server.cert'),
};

app.get('/', (req, res) => {
  res.send('Secure Hello, world!');
});

https.createServer(options, app).listen(3000, ()
=> {
  console.log('HTTPS    server    running    on
https://localhost:3000');
```

```
});
```

This sets up an HTTPS server that listens on port 3000.

2. Redirect HTTP to HTTPS

To ensure that users always use HTTPS, redirect HTTP traffic to HTTPS:

```javascript
const http = require('http');

http.createServer((req, res) => {
  res.redirect('https://' + req.headers.host + req.url);
}).listen(80);
```

Security Headers and Preventing Cross-Site Scripting (XSS)

Setting the correct **HTTP security headers** can prevent various attacks, including **XSS** and **clickjacking**.

1. Common Security Headers

- **Content-Security-Policy (CSP)**: Defines which resources are allowed to be loaded. This is the most important defense against XSS attacks.

- **X-Frame-Options**: Prevents your site from being embedded in an iframe (protects against clickjacking).
- **Strict-Transport-Security (HSTS)**: Forces browsers to always use HTTPS.

Example of setting security headers using **Helmet**:

javascript

```
const express = require('express');
const helmet = require('helmet');
const app = express();

app.use(helmet()); // Use helmet to set various
security headers

app.get('/', (req, res) => {
  res.send('Hello, world!');
});

app.listen(3000, () => {
  console.log('App          running          on
https://localhost:3000');
});
```

Real-World Example: Hardening an API Against Attacks

Let's harden a simple **Express API** against common security vulnerabilities.

Step 1: Use Helmet for Basic Security

javascript

```javascript
const express = require('express');
const helmet = require('helmet');
const app = express();

app.use(helmet()); // Set security headers
```

Step 2: Enable HTTPS

Use the `https` module to secure your API with SSL/TLS encryption.

javascript

```javascript
const https = require('https');
const fs = require('fs');

const options = {
  key: fs.readFileSync('server.key'),
  cert: fs.readFileSync('server.cert'),
};
```

```
https.createServer(options, app).listen(3000, ()
=> {
  console.log('Secure      API      running      on
https://localhost:3000');
});
```

Step 3: Preventing XSS

Sanitize user input using **DOMPurify** and always escape dynamic content.

javascript

```
const DOMPurify = require('dompurify');

app.post('/user', (req, res) => {
  const username = req.body.username;
  const               safeUsername              =
DOMPurify.sanitize(username);
  res.send(`Welcome, ${safeUsername}`);
});
```

Step 4: Implementing CSRF Protection

Use **csurf** middleware to prevent Cross-Site Request Forgery (CSRF).

javascript

```
const csrf = require('csurf');
const csrfProtection = csrf({ cookie: true });
```

```
app.use(csrfProtection);

app.get('/form', (req, res) => {
  res.render('form',          {          csrfToken:
req.csrfToken() });
});
```

Step 5: Secure API Endpoints

Ensure sensitive routes are protected with authentication, and use rate limiting to prevent abuse.

Conclusion

In this chapter, we learned about **security best practices** for securing **Node.js applications**. We discussed common web security vulnerabilities, such as **XSS**, **SQL injection**, and **CSRF**, and how to mitigate these risks using tools like **Helmet, HTTPS**, and **anti-CSRF tokens**. We also demonstrated how to harden an **Express API** against attacks by using security headers, encryption, and input sanitization.

Securing your Node.js applications is crucial to protect both your users and your system from potential threats. In the next chapter, we will discuss **performance optimization** strategies to ensure your applications are fast and scalable.

CHAPTER 21

WORKING WITH APIS IN NODE.JS

Node.js makes it easy to interact with external APIs and consume data from them. Whether you're building a web application, a mobile app backend, or integrating third-party services, understanding how to work with APIs in Node.js is a must-have skill. In this chapter, we'll learn how to consume external APIs using **Axios** and **Fetch**, handle API responses and errors, and go through a **real-world example** of integrating a **third-party weather API**.

Consuming External APIs with Axios

Axios is one of the most popular libraries for making HTTP requests in Node.js. It is promise-based, which makes it easier to handle asynchronous operations. Axios simplifies making HTTP requests and processing responses in both the client-side and server-side environments.

1. Installing Axios

To use Axios in a Node.js project, you first need to install it via npm:

```bash
bash
```

```bash
npm install axios --save
```

2. Making a GET Request with Axios

Here's an example of making a simple **GET** request using Axios to fetch data from an API:

```javascript
javascript
```

```javascript
const axios = require('axios');

// Example API URL (JSONPlaceholder is a free
fake online REST API)
const                    apiURL              =
'https://jsonplaceholder.typicode.com/posts';

axios.get(apiURL)
    .then(response => {
        console.log('Data              fetched:',
response.data);
    })
    .catch(error => {
```

```
      console.error('Error    fetching    data:',
error);
    });
```

In this example:

- **axios.get()** sends a GET request to the specified URL.
- **then()** handles the successful response, logging the fetched data.
- **catch()** handles any errors that occur during the request.

3. Making a POST Request with Axios

To send data to an API (using the POST method), you can use axios.post().

javascript

```
const axios = require('axios');

const                    apiURL                    =
'https://jsonplaceholder.typicode.com/posts';
const postData = {
    title: 'foo',
    body: 'bar',
    userId: 1
};

axios.post(apiURL, postData)
```

```
.then(response => {
    console.log('Response    from    POST:',
response.data);
    })
    .catch(error => {
    console.error('Error in POST request:',
error);
    });
```

In this example:

- **axios.post()** sends a POST request to the specified URL with the postData object.
- The server response is logged upon success.

Making API Requests with Fetch

Fetch is another popular option for making API requests. While it's more commonly used in the browser, with the help of the node-fetch package, you can use it in Node.js as well.

1. Installing Node Fetch

To use Fetch in Node.js, you need to install **node-fetch**:

bash

```
npm install node-fetch --save
```

2. Making a GET Request with Fetch

Once you have installed `node-fetch`, you can use it to make requests similarly to Axios:

```javascript
const fetch = require('node-fetch');

const apiURL = 'https://jsonplaceholder.typicode.com/posts';

fetch(apiURL)
    .then(response => response.json())
    .then(data => {
        console.log('Data fetched:', data);
    })
    .catch(error => {
        console.error('Error fetching data:', error);
    });
```

In this example:

- **fetch()** sends a GET request to the specified URL.
- The response is converted to JSON using `.json()`.
- The data is logged upon a successful response.

3. Making a POST Request with Fetch

Here's how you can send data with the POST method using **Fetch**:

javascript

```javascript
const fetch = require('node-fetch');

const apiURL = 'https://jsonplaceholder.typicode.com/posts';
const postData = {
    title: 'foo',
    body: 'bar',
    userId: 1
};

fetch(apiURL, {
    method: 'POST',
    headers: {
        'Content-Type': 'application/json',
    },
    body: JSON.stringify(postData)
})
    .then(response => response.json())
    .then(data => {
        console.log('Response from POST:', data);
    })
    .catch(error => {
```

```
    console.error('Error in POST request:',
error);
    });
```

In this example:

- We specify the **method** as POST.

- The **headers** include `'Content-Type':` `'application/json'` to indicate that we are sending JSON data.

- The **body** is the payload that will be sent, converted to a string with `JSON.stringify()`.

Handling API Responses and Errors

Whether you're using **Axios** or **Fetch**, handling **API responses** and **errors** properly is essential for building reliable applications.

1. Handling Successful API Responses

When an API request is successful, you typically receive data in the response. You should handle the data appropriately by checking the response status and parsing the response body.

For Axios, you can access the response data directly via `response.data`:

```javascript
```

```javascript
axios.get('https://jsonplaceholder.typicode.com
/posts')
    .then(response => {
        console.log('API           Response:',
response.data);
    })
    .catch(error => {
        console.error('Error:', error);
    });
```

For Fetch, you need to check if the response is successful (i.e., status code 200) before parsing the body:

```javascript
```

```javascript
fetch('https://jsonplaceholder.typicode.com/pos
ts')
    .then(response => {
        if (!response.ok) {
            throw new Error('Network response
was not ok');
        }
        return response.json();
    })
    .then(data => {
        console.log('API Response:', data);
    })
    .catch(error => {
```

```
        console.error('Error:', error);
    });
```

2. Handling API Errors

Handling errors in API calls is important for maintaining a stable user experience. You should catch errors related to network issues, server errors, and data errors.

For Axios:

javascript

```
axios.get('https://jsonplaceholder.typicode.com
/nonexistent')
    .then(response => {
        console.log(response.data);
    })
    .catch(error => {
        console.error('Error   fetching   data:',
error.message);
    });
```

For Fetch:

javascript

```
fetch('https://jsonplaceholder.typicode.com/non
existent')
    .then(response => {
```

275

```
    if (!response.ok) {
        throw new Error('API not found');
    }
    return response.json();
})
.then(data => {
    console.log(data);
})
.catch(error => {
    console.error('Error:', error.message);
});
```

In both examples, errors are caught in the .catch() block, and the error messages are logged.

Real-World Example: Integrating a Third-Party Weather API

Let's integrate a **third-party weather API** (such as the **OpenWeatherMap API**) into a Node.js app. We'll fetch the weather data for a given city and handle both the API response and any errors.

Step 1: Get an API Key

First, sign up for an API key at **OpenWeatherMap**: https://openweathermap.org/api.

Step 2: Install Axios

If you haven't installed Axios yet, do so now:

bash

```
npm install axios --save
```

Step 3: Create the Weather Fetching Function

Create a function to fetch the weather data using the **Axios** library:

javascript

```
const axios = require('axios');

// Replace this with your OpenWeatherMap API key
const apiKey = 'your-api-key';
const                baseURL                =
'http://api.openweathermap.org/data/2.5/weather
';

function getWeather(city) {
    const                url                =
`${baseURL}?q=${city}&appid=${apiKey}&units=met
ric`;

    axios.get(url)
        .then(response => {
            const data = response.data;
```

```
          console.log(`The       weather       in
${data.name}                                  is
${data.weather[0].description}.`);
          console.log(`Temperature:
${data.main.temp}°C`);
      })
      .catch(error => {
          console.error('Error          fetching
weather      data:',      error.response      ?
error.response.data : error.message);
      });
}


// Test the function with a city
getWeather('London');
```

Step 4: Running the Application

Run the script, and you should see the current weather for **London** (or the city of your choice) printed in the console.

Conclusion

In this chapter, we learned how to work with **APIs** in Node.js using libraries like **Axios** and **Fetch**. We covered how to make both **GET** and **POST** requests, handle **API responses** and **errors**, and discussed how to integrate a **third-party weather API** in a real-world example. By using these tools and techniques, you can easily integrate external APIs into your Node.js applications to fetch data and perform useful operations.

In the next chapter, we will dive deeper into **real-time communication** with WebSockets and how to implement **real-time features** in your applications.

CHAPTER 22

INTEGRATING FRONTEND WITH NODE.JS (FULL-STACK DEVELOPMENT)

In this chapter, we will explore how **Node.js** can be used to build **full-stack web applications** by integrating with popular frontend frameworks such as **React**, **Angular**, and **Vue.js**. Additionally, we'll cover serving static files with **Express** and using **template engines** like **EJS**, **Pug**, and **Handlebars** to render dynamic HTML pages. Finally, we'll go through a **real-world example** of building a simple **full-stack web application**.

How Node.js Works with Frontend Frameworks (React, Angular, Vue)

Node.js is primarily a backend runtime environment, but it plays a key role in full-stack development by serving the backend logic, APIs, and handling requests. On the frontend side, modern JavaScript frameworks such as **React**, **Angular**, and **Vue.js** are used to build interactive user interfaces.

1. Node.js with React

React is a popular frontend library for building user interfaces, especially single-page applications (SPAs). In full-stack applications, React interacts with Node.js through **APIs** that are provided by the backend.

- **React Frontend**: React components are responsible for rendering the UI.
- **Node.js Backend**: Node.js serves the backend API endpoints (e.g., using **Express**) that React calls via **HTTP requests**.

For a React-Node.js full-stack app:

- **React** will handle the rendering of the UI and call APIs from the **Node.js** backend using **Axios** or **Fetch**.
- **Node.js** will manage the business logic, serve APIs, and interact with databases.

2. Node.js with Angular

Angular is a comprehensive frontend framework built by Google, often used for building large-scale, enterprise-level applications.

- **Angular Frontend**: Angular manages the frontend application using components, services, and routing.

281

- **Node.js Backend**: Angular makes HTTP requests to Node.js APIs, similar to React.

In an Angular-Node.js full-stack setup:

- **Angular** provides the user interface and communicates with the **Node.js** server through HTTP requests.
- **Node.js** provides the backend APIs, which **Angular** uses to fetch and manipulate data.

3. Node.js with Vue.js

Vue.js is a progressive framework for building user interfaces. It can also serve as the view layer in a full-stack application, similar to React and Angular.

- **Vue Frontend**: Vue.js creates reactive user interfaces and interacts with backend APIs.
- **Node.js Backend**: Node.js serves as the API provider.

For a Vue.js-Node.js full-stack setup:

- **Vue.js** components handle the dynamic aspects of the UI.
- **Node.js** provides the necessary API endpoints to process data requests from the **Vue.js** app.

Serving Static Files with Express

In a full-stack Node.js application, static files (like images, CSS, and JavaScript files) need to be served by the backend. **Express** makes it easy to serve these files using the **express.static** middleware.

1. Using express.static Middleware

- **Static files** are typically stored in a public directory, such as **/public**.
- **Express** can serve files from this directory by specifying it as a static folder.

Example:

```javascript
const express = require('express');
const app = express();
const path = require('path');

// Serve static files from the 'public' directory
app.use(express.static(path.join(__dirname, 'public')));

app.get('/', (req, res) => {
  res.sendFile(path.join(__dirname,    'public', 'index.html'));
```

```
});

app.listen(3000, () => {
  console.log('Server          running          on
http://localhost:3000');
});
```

In this example:

- The **express.static** middleware serves static files (like CSS, JS, and images) from the `public` folder.
- The root route sends the `index.html` file to the client.

2. Organizing Static Files

- **Images**: Store images in a subdirectory like `/images`.
- **CSS/JS**: Store stylesheets and scripts in `/css` and `/js` respectively.

Template Engines: EJS, Pug, Handlebars

Template engines are used in Node.js to dynamically generate HTML pages by embedding data within HTML templates. These engines allow you to send dynamic content (from the backend) to the client's browser.

1. EJS (Embedded JavaScript)

EJS is a simple templating engine that lets you embed JavaScript code into HTML files.

- **Installing EJS**:

```bash
npm install ejs --save
```

- **Using EJS** in an Express app:

```javascript
const express = require('express');
const app = express();

// Set EJS as the view engine
app.set('view engine', 'ejs');

// Define a route to render an EJS template
app.get('/', (req, res) => {
  res.render('index', { title: 'Node.js
with EJS' });
});

app.listen(3000, () => {
  console.log('Server      running      on
http://localhost:3000');
```

285

```
});
```

- **index.ejs** (template):

```
html

<html>
  <head>
    <title><%= title %></title>
  </head>
  <body>
    <h1>Welcome to <%= title %>!</h1>
  </body>
</html>
```

In this example, **EJS** renders an HTML page with dynamic data (the `title`).

2. Pug (formerly Jade)

Pug is a high-performance template engine for Node.js that uses indentation-based syntax for templating.

- **Installing Pug**:

```bash
npm install pug --save
```

- **Using Pug** in Express:

286

```javascript
const express = require('express');
const app = express();

// Set Pug as the view engine
app.set('view engine', 'pug');

// Define a route to render a Pug template
app.get('/', (req, res) => {
  res.render('index', { title: 'Node.js with Pug' });
});

app.listen(3000, () => {
  console.log('Server      running      on http://localhost:3000');
});
```

- **index.pug** (template):

```pug
doctype html
html
  head
    title #{title}
  body
    h1 Welcome to #{title}!
```

287

3. Handlebars

Handlebars is a popular templating engine that provides more powerful features, such as helpers and custom functions, to customize the templates.

- **Installing Handlebars**:

bash

```
npm install handlebars --save
```

- **Using Handlebars** in Express:

javascript

```
const express = require('express');
const handlebars = require('express-
handlebars');
const app = express();

// Set Handlebars as the view engine
app.engine('handlebars', handlebars());
app.set('view engine', 'handlebars');

// Define a route to render a Handlebars
template
app.get('/', (req, res) => {
  res.render('home', { title: 'Node.js
with Handlebars' });
```

288

```
});

app.listen(3000, () => {
  console.log('Server          running          on
http://localhost:3000');
});
```

- **home.handlebars** (template):

```
handlebars
```

```
<html>
  <head>
    <title>{{title}}</title>
  </head>
  <body>
    <h1>Welcome to {{title}}!</h1>
  </body>
</html>
```

Real-World Example: Building a Full-Stack Web Application

Let's build a **full-stack application** that uses **React** on the frontend and **Express** on the backend. This example will allow users to submit a form, and the data will be displayed in the frontend.

Step 1: Backend (Node.js/Express API)

1. Set up a basic **Express** API:

bash

```bash
mkdir fullstack-app
cd fullstack-app
npm init -y
npm install express body-parser cors --save
```

2. Create the app.js file:

javascript

```javascript
const express = require('express');
const bodyParser = require('body-parser');
const cors = require('cors');
const app = express();

// Middleware
app.use(cors());
app.use(bodyParser.json());

// Store user data (in-memory for
simplicity)
const users = [];

// API endpoint to get all users
app.get('/api/users', (req, res) => {
```

290

```
    res.json(users);
  });


  // API endpoint to add a new user
  app.post('/api/users', (req, res) => {
    const user = req.body;
    users.push(user);
    res.status(201).json(user);
  });


  app.listen(3001, () => {
    console.log('Backend server running on
  http://localhost:3001');
  });
```

Step 2: Frontend (React)

1. Create a React app:

```bash
npx create-react-app frontend
cd frontend
npm start
```

2. Create a simple form and display the user data in **App.js**:

```javascript
import React, { useState, useEffect } from
'react';
```

291

```
function App() {
  const [users, setUsers] = useState([]);
  const [name, setName] = useState('');

  // Fetch users from the backend API
  useEffect(() => {

fetch('http://localhost:3001/api/users')
      .then((response) => response.json())
      .then((data) => setUsers(data));
  }, []);

  // Handle form submission
  const handleSubmit = (e) => {
    e.preventDefault();

fetch('http://localhost:3001/api/users', {
      method: 'POST',
      headers:      {      'Content-Type':
'application/json' },
      body: JSON.stringify({ name }),
    })
      .then((response) => response.json())
      .then((newUser)                    =>
setUsers([...users, newUser]));
  };

  return (
```

```
<div className="App">
  <h1>Users</h1>
  <form onSubmit={handleSubmit}>
    <input
      type="text"
      value={name}
      onChange={(e)                       =>
setName(e.target.value)}
      placeholder="Enter name"
    />
    <button            type="submit">Add
User</button>
  </form>
  <ul>
    {users.map((user, index) => (
      <li key={index}>{user.name}</li>
    ))}
  </ul>
</div>
  );
}

export default App;
```

Conclusion

In this chapter, we explored how to integrate **Node.js** with various **frontend frameworks** like **React**, **Angular**, and **Vue**. We also covered how to serve **static files** with **Express** and use **template engines** like **EJS**, **Pug**, and **Handlebars** for rendering dynamic HTML. Finally, we walked through a **real-world example** of building a simple **full-stack web application** using **React** as the frontend and **Express** as the backend.

With this knowledge, you can now build full-stack applications, integrate frontend and backend technologies, and deliver dynamic, interactive web experiences.

CHAPTER 23

ADVANCED NODE.JS PATTERNS AND BEST PRACTICES

As your Node.js applications grow in size and complexity, it becomes important to adopt advanced coding patterns and best practices to keep your codebase **scalable, maintainable,** and **efficient**. In this chapter, we will dive into **modularizing your Node.js code**, explore some **design patterns** in Node.js, and discuss strategies for building **scalable and maintainable applications**. We will conclude with a **real-world example** of building a **scalable e-commerce application** using these techniques.

Modularizing Your Node.js Code

One of the best practices for building scalable and maintainable applications is to **modularize** your code. Modularization refers to the practice of breaking your application into small, reusable pieces (modules), each of which performs a specific task. This makes the code more **manageable, testable,** and **scalable**.

1. Benefits of Modularizing Code

- **Reusability**: Code that is separated into smaller, reusable modules can be shared across different parts of the application.

- **Readability**: Smaller modules make the code easier to understand and maintain.

- **Testability**: Modules can be tested independently, which is crucial for unit testing.

- **Scalability**: As the application grows, new modules can be added without affecting the existing structure.

2. How to Modularize Node.js Code

In Node.js, modules are created by **separating functionality** into individual files and **exporting** them for use in other parts of the application.

Example: Modularizing an Express application

- **Creating a Module (user.js)**:

```javascript

// user.js (model)
const users = [];

function addUser(name) {
    const user = { name };
```

```
    users.push(user);
    return user;
}


function getUsers() {
    return users;
}


module.exports = { addUser, getUsers };
```

- **Using the Module in app.js**:

```javascript
const express = require('express');
const app = express();
const { addUser, getUsers } = require('./user');

app.get('/add-user', (req, res) => {
    const user = addUser('John Doe');
    res.send(user);
});

app.get('/users', (req, res) => {
    const allUsers = getUsers();
    res.json(allUsers);
});

app.listen(3000, () => {
```

297

```
    console.log('Server  running  on  port
3000');
});
```

Here, we've split the user-related logic into the `user.js` module. This makes the code more organized and easier to scale.

Design Patterns in Node.js

In software development, design patterns are proven solutions to common problems. Applying design patterns in Node.js applications can help you write code that is **easy to maintain**, **extensible**, and **robust**.

1. Common Design Patterns in Node.js

- **Module Pattern**: Used for organizing code into reusable components (like the example above with `user.js`).
- **Singleton Pattern**: Ensures that a class has only one instance and provides a global point of access.
- **Observer Pattern**: Allows an object (subject) to notify other objects (observers) of any changes, often used in event-driven systems.
- **Factory Pattern**: Used for creating objects without specifying the exact class of object that will be created, ideal for handling complex object creation.

298

- **Middleware Pattern**: In Express, middleware functions allow you to modify requests, responses, and route handling by layering functionality in a modular way.

2. Example: Singleton Pattern

In Node.js, the **Singleton pattern** is commonly used when you need to manage **shared resources** (e.g., database connections) and ensure only one instance of an object exists.

Example: Singleton Database Connection

```javascript
// db.js (singleton)
const { MongoClient } = require('mongodb');

class Database {
  constructor() {
    if (!Database.instance) {
      Database.instance = this;
      this.client                =              new
MongoClient('mongodb://localhost:27017');
      this.db = null;
    }
    return Database.instance;
  }

  async connect() {
```

```
    if (!this.db) {
      await this.client.connect();
      this.db = this.client.db('mydatabase');
    }
    return this.db;
  }
}


module.exports = new Database();
```

In this example:

- The `Database` class is designed as a **singleton**, ensuring only one instance of the database connection is created.
- We use the `connect()` method to establish a connection to the database, but the same instance is reused if already connected.

Building Scalable and Maintainable Applications

Building scalable and maintainable applications in Node.js involves adhering to several **best practices** and applying patterns that support growth.

1. Separation of Concerns

To build a scalable app, you need to keep your application's components independent of each other. This can be achieved by:

- **Dividing your application into layers**: Separate business logic, routes, and models.

- **Using MVC (Model-View-Controller) architecture**: Separate your application's logic into three main components: Models (data), Views (UI), and Controllers (business logic).

2. Error Handling and Logging

Proper error handling and logging are essential for maintaining a scalable application. Use structured error handling with proper error messages, and implement logging to monitor application health.

Example:

javascript

```javascript
// Middleware for handling errors
app.use((err, req, res, next) => {
    console.error(err.stack);
    res.status(500).send('Something broke!');
});
```

For logging, use libraries like **Winston** or **Morgan**:

bash

```bash
npm install winston morgan --save
```

301

```javascript
const morgan = require('morgan');
const winston = require('winston');

app.use(morgan('combined'));
const logger = winston.createLogger({
  transports: [
    new winston.transports.Console(),
    new    winston.transports.File({    filename:
'app.log' })
  ]
});
```

3. Database Scalability

When dealing with a growing amount of data, ensure that your database is optimized and scalable:

- **Use indexes** to speed up queries.
- **Consider sharding** if your data grows too large to fit on a single server.
- **Use pagination** to handle large datasets efficiently.

4. Caching for Scalability

Implement caching mechanisms (e.g., using **Redis**) to store frequently accessed data, reducing the load on databases and improving response time.

5. Asynchronous Programming

Node.js is built to handle asynchronous operations efficiently, but you should avoid blocking code to ensure your app scales well:

- Use **Promises** or **async/await** to handle asynchronous tasks.
- Leverage **worker threads** or **child processes** for CPU-intensive tasks.

Real-World Example: A Scalable E-commerce Application

Let's build a scalable e-commerce application with **Express** that follows best practices.

1. Application Structure

For a scalable e-commerce app, we can organize the files using an **MVC** structure:

bash

```
/e-commerce-app
    /models
        product.js
        user.js
    /controllers
        productController.js
```

303

```
        userController.js
    /routes
        productRoutes.js
        userRoutes.js
    /views
        productView.ejs
    /middlewares
        authMiddleware.js
    app.js
```

2. Example Model (product.js)

```
javascript
```

```javascript
// models/product.js
const mongoose = require('mongoose');

const productSchema = new mongoose.Schema({
    name: String,
    price: Number,
    description: String,
    stock: Number,
});

module.exports     =     mongoose.model('Product',
productSchema);
```

3. Example Controller (productController.js)

```
javascript
```

```javascript
// controllers/productController.js
const Product = require('../models/product');
```

```javascript
async function getProducts(req, res) {
    try {
        const products = await Product.find();
        res.render('productView', { products });
    } catch (err) {
        res.status(500).send('Error     fetching
products');
    }
}

async function addProduct(req, res) {
    const { name, price, description, stock } =
req.body;
    const newProduct = new Product({ name, price,
description, stock });
    await newProduct.save();
    res.redirect('/products');
}

module.exports = { getProducts, addProduct };
```

4. Example Routes (productRoutes.js)

javascript

```javascript
// routes/productRoutes.js
const express = require('express');
const router = express.Router();
const { getProducts, addProduct } =
require('../controllers/productController');
```

```
router.get('/products', getProducts);
router.post('/products', addProduct);

module.exports = router;
```

5. Example Middleware (authMiddleware.js)

javascript

```
// middlewares/authMiddleware.js
function isAuthenticated(req, res, next) {
    if (!req.isAuthenticated()) {
        return   res.status(401).send('You   must
log in first');
    }
    next();
}

module.exports = { isAuthenticated };
```

6. Main Application (app.js)

javascript

```
// app.js
const express = require('express');
const mongoose = require('mongoose');
const              productRoutes              =
require('./routes/productRoutes');
const    {    isAuthenticated    }    =
require('./middlewares/authMiddleware');
```

306

```
const app = express();
mongoose.connect('mongodb://localhost/ecommerce
-app');

app.use(express.json());
app.use(express.urlencoded({ extended: true }));

app.use('/', productRoutes);

// Example of securing routes with authentication
middleware
app.get('/admin', isAuthenticated, (req, res) =>
{
    res.send('Admin dashboard');
});

app.listen(3000, () => {
    console.log('Server   is   running   on   port
3000');
});
```

Conclusion

In this chapter, we explored **advanced Node.js patterns and best practices** to build **scalable** and **maintainable** applications. We discussed:

- **Modularizing your Node.js code** for better organization and reusability.
- Applying **design patterns** like **Singleton**, **Observer**, and **Factory** to handle common issues.
- **Building scalable applications** using MVC architecture, error handling, logging, and database optimization.

Finally, we went through a **real-world example** of building a **scalable e-commerce application** using best practices.

In the next chapter, we'll discuss **Node.js security best practices** and how to secure your application against common vulnerabilities.

CHAPTER 24

WORKING WITH

MICROSERVICES IN NODE.JS

Microservices architecture is an approach to software design where an application is broken down into smaller, independent services that can be developed, deployed, and scaled independently. In this chapter, we will explore **microservices** and how to implement them using **Node.js** and **Express**. We'll discuss the benefits of microservices, how to build and communicate between them, and wrap up with a **real-world example** of building a **microservice-based payment system**.

Introduction to Microservices Architecture

In traditional **monolithic** architectures, an application is built as a single unified unit, where all components are tightly coupled. While this works for smaller applications, it becomes harder to manage, scale, and maintain as the application grows.

Microservices architecture addresses this by breaking the application into small, independently deployable services. Each service is responsible for a specific piece of functionality, such as

309

user authentication, payment processing, or inventory management. These services communicate with each other over a network (usually via **HTTP APIs**, **REST**, or **gRPC**).

Benefits of Microservices:

1. **Scalability**: Individual microservices can be scaled independently based on demand.
2. **Flexibility**: Services can be written in different programming languages, allowing teams to use the best tools for the job.
3. **Resilience**: Failure in one service doesn't necessarily affect the entire application.
4. **Faster Development**: Teams can work on different services simultaneously, leading to faster development cycles.
5. **Easy Maintenance**: Since services are small, it's easier to update or refactor them without impacting other parts of the system.

Challenges of Microservices:

- **Complexity**: Managing and monitoring multiple services can be complex.
- **Data Management**: Managing data consistency across services can be challenging, especially when using different databases.

- **Communication Overhead**: Communication between services introduces network latency and can lead to failures if not handled properly.

Building Microservices with Node.js and Express

Node.js, with its event-driven and non-blocking architecture, is well-suited for building microservices. **Express** is a popular web framework for building lightweight APIs that make it easy to develop microservices.

1. Setting Up a Basic Microservice with Express

Let's create a simple **User Service** that exposes an API endpoint to retrieve user information.

1. **Install Node.js and Express**:

   bash

   ```
   mkdir user-service
   cd user-service
   npm init -y
   npm install express --save
   ```

2. **Create app.js for the User Service**:

   javascript

```javascript
const express = require('express');
const app = express();

// Dummy user data
const users = [
    { id: 1, name: 'Alice' },
    { id: 2, name: 'Bob' },
    { id: 3, name: 'Charlie' },
];

// Endpoint to get user by ID
app.get('/users/:id', (req, res) => {
    const              userId              =
parseInt(req.params.id);
    const user = users.find(u => u.id ===
userId);

    if (user) {
        res.json(user);
    } else {
        res.status(404).send('User      not
found');
    }
});

app.listen(3001, () => {
    console.log('User  Service  running  on
http://localhost:3001');
```

312

```
});
```

This basic microservice exposes an endpoint to retrieve a user by ID. It runs on port **3001**.

2. Creating Another Microservice (Order Service)

Next, let's create a second service, an **Order Service**, which communicates with the User Service to retrieve user details and order information.

1. **Install Express for Order Service**:

```bash
mkdir order-service
cd order-service
npm init -y
npm install express axios --save
```

2. **Create app.js for the Order Service**:

```javascript
const express = require('express');
const axios = require('axios');
const app = express();

// Define the base URL for the User Service
```

313

```
const              userServiceUrl       =
'http://localhost:3001/users';


// Endpoint to get order details along with
user info
app.get('/order/:userId', async (req, res)
=> {
    const userId = req.params.userId;

    try {
        // Fetch user data from User
Service
        const userResponse = await
axios.get(`${userServiceUrl}/${userId}`);
        const user = userResponse.data;

        // Dummy order data
        const order = {
            userId: user.id,
            orderId: 12345,
            product: 'Laptop',
            quantity: 1,
            totalPrice: 1500,
        };

        // Send response combining user
data and order data
        res.json({
            user,
```

```
        order,
    });
  } catch (error) {
      res.status(404).send('User      not
found');
  }
});


app.listen(3002, () => {
    console.log('Order Service running on
http://localhost:3002');
});
```

In this example:

- The **Order Service** calls the **User Service** using **Axios** to get user details.
- The **Order Service** combines user information with order data and returns it to the client.

3. Running the Microservices

Now, you can run both services in separate terminals:

1. Start the **User Service**:

```bash
node app.js
```

315

2. Start the **Order Service**:

```bash
```

```
node app.js
```

3. Visit the order service endpoint:
   - **http://localhost:3002/order/1** — This should fetch the user data from the **User Service** and combine it with order data from the **Order Service**.

Communication Between Microservices

Microservices communicate with each other over the network. Typically, they use **HTTP REST APIs**, but other communication mechanisms like **gRPC**, **message queues** (e.g., **RabbitMQ** or **Kafka**), or **WebSockets** can also be used.

1. Synchronous Communication (REST API)

In the example above, the **Order Service** makes a synchronous HTTP request to the **User Service** using **Axios**. This is the most common pattern in microservices communication.

316

2. Asynchronous Communication (Message Queues)

For decoupled services and better fault tolerance, microservices can communicate asynchronously using message queues. Services send messages to a queue, and other services listen for and process those messages.

Example with **RabbitMQ** (simplified):

- **Producer Service** sends a message to the queue.
- **Consumer Service** listens to the queue and processes the message.

```javascript
const amqp = require('amqplib/callback_api');

// Producer (send message)
amqp.connect('amqp://localhost', (error0,
connection) => {
  if (error0) throw error0;
  connection.createChannel((error1, channel) =>
{
    if (error1) throw error1;
    const queue = 'order_queue';
    const msg = 'New order placed';

    channel.assertQueue(queue, { durable: false
});
```

317

```
   channel.sendToQueue(queue,
Buffer.from(msg));
   console.log("Sent:", msg);
  });
});
```

Real-World Example: A Microservice-Based Payment System

Let's now build a **payment microservice** that processes payments. This example will consist of a **Payment Service** and a **User Service**.

1. Setting Up the Payment Service

In a real-world scenario, the **Payment Service** will handle payment processing by communicating with external payment gateways. For this example, we will simulate payment processing.

- **Install dependencies**:

  ```bash
  bash
  
  npm init -y
  npm install express axios body-parser --save
  ```

- **Create paymentService.js**:

  ```javascript
  javascript
  ```

318

```javascript
const express = require('express');
const axios = require('axios');
const app = express();
const bodyParser = require('body-parser');

app.use(bodyParser.json());

// Simulated external API for processing
payments
app.post('/process-payment', async (req,
res) => {
    const { userId, amount } = req.body;

    try {
        // Simulate a payment processing
request
        const paymentResponse = await
axios.post('http://payment-
gateway.com/pay', { userId, amount });

        res.status(200).json({
            message: 'Payment processed
successfully',
            paymentDetails:
paymentResponse.data,
        });
    } catch (error) {
```

```
        res.status(500).json({        error:
'Payment processing failed' });
    }
});

app.listen(3003, () => {
    console.log('Payment   Service   running
on http://localhost:3003');
});
```

2. Integrating the Payment Service with the Order Service

The **Order Service** will now interact with the **Payment Service** when an order is placed.

```javascript

const express = require('express');
const axios = require('axios');
const app = express();
app.use(express.json());

app.post('/place-order', async (req, res) => {
    const { userId, orderDetails } = req.body;

    try {
        // Call Payment Service to process the
payment
```

```
        const     paymentResponse    =     await
axios.post('http://localhost:3003/process-
payment', {
        userId,
        amount: orderDetails.totalPrice,
    });

    res.status(200).json({
        message:         'Order       placed
successfully',
        paymentDetails:
paymentResponse.data,
    });
  } catch (error) {
    res.status(500).send('Error      placing
order');
  }
});

app.listen(3002, () => {
  console.log('Order  Service  running  on
http://localhost:3002');
});
```

Now, the **Order Service** will call the **Payment Service** to process the payment whenever an order is placed.

Conclusion

In this chapter, we introduced **microservices architecture** and explored how to implement microservices with **Node.js** and **Express**. We discussed the benefits of microservices, how to build and communicate between microservices, and tackled the challenges of managing distributed services. We also built a **microservice-based payment system** as a real-world example, integrating multiple services and demonstrating how they communicate with each other.

Microservices offer significant advantages for large-scale applications, such as **scalability**, **resilience**, and **flexibility**. In the next chapter, we will focus on **performance optimization** techniques to ensure your Node.js applications perform efficiently in production.

CHAPTER 25

BUILDING GRAPHQL APIS WITH NODE.JS

In this chapter, we will explore **GraphQL**, an alternative to REST for building APIs. We will learn how to set up **Apollo Server** with **Node.js** to build GraphQL APIs, and how to perform **queries** and **mutations** to retrieve and modify data. Finally, we will build a **real-world example** of a **GraphQL API** for a **blogging platform**.

What is GraphQL?

GraphQL is a query language for your API, and a runtime for executing those queries with your existing data. It was developed by Facebook in 2012 and released as an open-source project in 2015. GraphQL allows clients to request only the data they need, and nothing more.

Key Features of GraphQL:

1. **Flexible Queries**: Clients can specify exactly what data they need, minimizing over-fetching or under-fetching.

2. **Single Endpoint**: Unlike REST APIs, which typically have multiple endpoints for different resources, GraphQL uses a single endpoint for all operations.

3. **Real-time Data**: With **subscriptions**, GraphQL can also provide real-time data updates to clients.

4. **Strongly Typed**: GraphQL schemas define types, ensuring that the data conforms to a specific structure.

How GraphQL Works:

- **Query**: Clients send queries to retrieve data.
- **Mutation**: Clients send mutations to modify data.
- **Schema**: Defines the types of data and operations (queries and mutations) that are available in the API.

Setting Up Apollo Server with Node.js

Apollo Server is a popular library for building a GraphQL server in **Node.js**. It provides a simple way to set up a GraphQL API and integrate it with your application.

1. Installing Apollo Server and Dependencies

To get started, we need to install **Apollo Server** and **GraphQL** in our Node.js project.

1. Initialize your project:

```bash
bash
```

```bash
mkdir graphql-blog-api
cd graphql-blog-api
npm init -y
```

2. Install dependencies:

```bash
bash
```

```bash
npm install apollo-server graphql --save
```

2. Creating a Basic Apollo Server

Create a file index.js to define the server and set up the GraphQL schema.

```javascript
javascript
```

```javascript
const { ApolloServer, gql } = require('apollo-server');

// Define the GraphQL schema using SDL (Schema Definition Language)
const typeDefs = gql`
  type Query {
    hello: String
  }
`;
```

```
// Define resolvers that handle the actual data
retrieval for the queries
const resolvers = {
  Query: {
    hello: () => 'Hello, GraphQL!',
  },
};


// Create an Apollo Server instance
const server = new ApolloServer({ typeDefs,
resolvers });


// Start the server
server.listen().then(({ url }) => {
  console.log(`Server ready at ${url}`);
});
```

In this basic example:

- We define a **Query** type with a `hello` field.
- The **resolver** for `hello` returns a simple string.
- Apollo Server is initialized, and the server is started.

To run the server, execute the following:

```bash
bash
```

```
node index.js
```

Visit the **GraphQL Playground** in your browser at `http://localhost:4000/` to interact with the API and run queries.

Querying and Mutating Data with GraphQL

GraphQL allows for **querying** and **mutating** data. **Queries** are used to fetch data, while **mutations** are used to create, update, or delete data.

1. Querying Data

To query data in GraphQL, you define **fields** in the query corresponding to fields in the **schema**. In the previous example, we defined a `hello` field in the `Query` type. We can query it like this:

```graphql
graphql

query {
  hello
}
```

This query will return the string "Hello, GraphQL!".

2. Mutating Data

Mutations are similar to queries but are used to modify data. Here's how to set up a **mutation** in GraphQL.

Example: Adding a Blog Post

1. **Extend the schema** to include a `BlogPost` type and a mutation for adding posts:

javascript

```javascript
const { ApolloServer, gql } = require('apollo-server');

let posts = [];

const typeDefs = gql`
  type BlogPost {
    id: ID
    title: String
    content: String
  }

  type Query {
    getPosts: [BlogPost]
  }

  type Mutation {
```

```
    addPost(title:  String,  content:  String):
BlogPost
  }
`;


const resolvers = {
  Query: {
    getPosts: () => posts,
  },
  Mutation: {
    addPost: (parent, args) => {
      const newPost = { id: posts.length + 1,
...args };
      posts.push(newPost);
      return newPost;
    },
  },
};


const server = new ApolloServer({ typeDefs,
resolvers });


server.listen().then(({ url }) => {
  console.log(`Server ready at ${url}`);
});
```

2. **Querying the Blog Posts**:

```
graphql
```

```
query {
  getPosts {
    id
    title
    content
  }
}
```

This query will return all the posts stored in the `posts` array.

3. **Mutating the Blog Posts**:

```
graphql

mutation {
  addPost(title: "GraphQL Basics", content:
"Learn how to use GraphQL with Node.js.") {
    id
    title
    content
  }
}
```

This mutation will add a new blog post and return the newly added post with its `id`, `title`, and `content`.

Real-World Example: Building a GraphQL API for a Blogging Platform

Now let's build a **GraphQL API** for a **blogging platform**. The API will allow us to:

- Query for all blog posts.
- Add new blog posts.
- Update blog posts.
- Delete blog posts.

1. Define the Schema

We will define a schema that includes:

- **Queries** to retrieve blog posts.
- **Mutations** to create, update, and delete blog posts.

```javascript
const { ApolloServer, gql } = require('apollo-server');

// Mock database
let posts = [
  { id: '1', title: 'Introduction to GraphQL', content: 'GraphQL is a powerful query language.' },
```

```
  { id: '2', title: 'Getting Started with
Node.js', content: 'Node.js is a JavaScript
runtime built on Chrome's V8 engine.' },
];

const typeDefs = gql`
  type BlogPost {
    id: ID!
    title: String!
    content: String!
  }

  type Query {
    getPosts: [BlogPost]
    getPost(id: ID!): BlogPost
  }

  type Mutation {
    addPost(title: String!, content: String!):
BlogPost
    updatePost(id: ID!, title: String, content:
String): BlogPost
    deletePost(id: ID!): BlogPost
  }
`;

const resolvers = {
  Query: {
    getPosts: () => posts,
```

```
      getPost: (parent, args) => posts.find(post =>
post.id === args.id),
    },
  Mutation: {
    addPost: (parent, args) => {
      const newPost = { id: String(posts.length
+ 1), title: args.title, content: args.content };
      posts.push(newPost);
      return newPost;
    },
    updatePost: (parent, args) => {
      let post = posts.find(post => post.id ===
args.id);
      if (post) {
        post = { ...post, ...args };
      }
      return post;
    },
    deletePost: (parent, args) => {
      const index = posts.findIndex(post =>
post.id === args.id);
      if (index !== -1) {
        return posts.splice(index, 1)[0];
      }
      return null;
    },
  },
};
```

```
const   server   =   new   ApolloServer({   typeDefs,
resolvers });
```

```
server.listen().then((({ url }) => {
  console.log(`Server ready at ${url}`);
});
```

2. Running the Server

Start the server by running:

```bash
```

```
node index.js
```

Visit **GraphQL Playground** at `http://localhost:4000/` to interact with the API.

3. Queries and Mutations

- **Get All Posts** (Query):

```graphql
```

```
query {
  getPosts {
    id
    title
    content
  }
}
```

334

- **Add a New Post** (Mutation):

```graphql
mutation {
  addPost(title: "GraphQL in Action",
content: "Learn advanced GraphQL
patterns.") {
    id
    title
    content
  }
}
```

- **Update a Post** (Mutation):

```graphql
mutation {
  updatePost(id: "1", title: "Advanced
GraphQL", content: "Learn advanced
features in GraphQL.") {
    id
    title
    content
  }
}
```

- **Delete a Post** (Mutation):

335

```
graphql

mutation {
  deletePost(id: "2") {
    id
    title
  }
}
```

Conclusion

In this chapter, we learned about **GraphQL** and how to build a **GraphQL API** using **Apollo Server** and **Node.js**. We covered:

- The basic concepts of **GraphQL**, including **queries**, **mutations**, and **schemas**.
- How to set up **Apollo Server** with **Node.js**.
- How to query and mutate data using GraphQL.
- A **real-world example** of building a **GraphQL API** for a **blogging platform**.

GraphQL allows for a more flexible and efficient way of interacting with APIs, especially when compared to traditional REST APIs. In the next chapter, we will dive into **real-time communication** with **WebSockets** and how to implement real-time features in your applications.

CHAPTER 26

SCALING NODE.JS APPLICATIONS

As your Node.js application grows, you'll need to address challenges related to performance, availability, and reliability. **Scaling** an application is crucial to handle increased traffic and ensure that your application can continue to perform well under heavy load. In this chapter, we will explore techniques for **scaling Node.js applications**, including **clustering**, **load balancing**, and using **Redis** for **session management**. Finally, we will look at a **real-world example** of scaling a **social media application**.

Clustering and Load Balancing

In Node.js, the **single-threaded nature** of the runtime means that a single process can only utilize one CPU core. As a result, a single Node.js process can only handle a limited number of requests concurrently. **Clustering** allows you to take advantage of multiple CPU cores to distribute the load and improve the performance of your application.

1. Clustering in Node.js

Node.js provides a **cluster** module that enables you to create multiple child processes (workers) that share the same server port. Each worker runs on a different core, which helps in utilizing multi-core systems.

Example: Simple Node.js Clustering

```javascript
const cluster = require('cluster');
const http = require('http');
const os = require('os');

const numCPUs = os.cpus().length;

if (cluster.isMaster) {
  // Fork workers for each CPU core
  for (let i = 0; i < numCPUs; i++) {
    cluster.fork();
  }

  cluster.on('exit', (worker, code, signal) => {
    console.log(`Worker   ${worker.process.pid}
died`);
  });
} else {
  // Workers share the same server port
```

```
http.createServer((req, res) => {
  res.writeHead(200);
  res.end('Hello, Node.js with Clustering!');
}).listen(8000);
}
```

In this example:

- **Master process** forks workers based on the number of available CPU cores.
- Each worker listens on the same port (8000), and the load is distributed across multiple workers.
- This enables the application to handle more requests simultaneously.

2. Load Balancing

While clustering allows you to scale across multiple CPU cores, **load balancing** ensures that incoming requests are evenly distributed across all available processes (workers).

- **Round-robin** is the most common load balancing technique. It sends incoming requests to workers in a circular order, ensuring that each worker gets an equal number of requests.

For production environments, you may want to use an **external load balancer** (e.g., **NGINX, HAProxy**, or **AWS Elastic Load**

Balancing) to distribute requests among multiple instances of your Node.js application running on different servers or containers.

Horizontal and Vertical Scaling

Scaling refers to the ability to add resources to your application in order to handle more traffic and workload. There are two main approaches to scaling applications:

1. Vertical Scaling (Scaling Up)

Vertical scaling involves **increasing the capacity** of a single server by upgrading its CPU, memory, or disk storage. This method is simple to implement, but it has limits and may become expensive at higher levels of capacity.

- **Pros**: Simple and cost-effective for small to medium applications.
- **Cons**: Limited scalability; once the server reaches its maximum capacity, you need to upgrade to an even more powerful machine.

2. Horizontal Scaling (Scaling Out)

Horizontal scaling involves **adding more servers** to distribute the load and increase application capacity. This can be achieved by running multiple instances of your application across different servers or containers. Horizontal scaling is more complex to set up but is more scalable and resilient.

- **Pros**: Can scale infinitely by adding more servers.
- **Cons**: Requires load balancing, managing multiple servers, and ensuring data consistency across instances.

Horizontal scaling is especially useful for high-traffic applications where traffic spikes are common.

Using Redis for Session Management

In a distributed system where multiple instances of your application are running (such as in horizontal scaling), maintaining consistent user sessions can be challenging. If a user is routed to different instances on each request, the session data will not persist unless it's stored in a **shared session store**.

Redis is an in-memory data store commonly used for session management in distributed applications because of its **fast read/write operations** and **ability to handle high volumes of concurrent requests**.

1. Setting Up Redis with Node.js

To use Redis for session management, first, you need to install **Redis** and a Node.js client like **ioredis** or **redis**.

Install **ioredis**:

```bash
bash
```

```bash
npm install ioredis --save
```

Install **express-session** for handling sessions:

```bash
bash
```

```bash
npm install express-session --save
```

2. Configuring Redis for Session Management

Here's how you can set up **Redis** to store session data for a Node.js application using **Express**.

```javascript
javascript

const express = require('express');
const session = require('express-session');
const Redis = require('ioredis');
const     RedisStore     =     require('connect-
redis')(session);

const app = express();
```

```
const redis = new Redis(); // Connect to Redis

// Configure session middleware with RedisStore
app.use(session({
  store: new RedisStore({ client: redis }),
  secret: 'my-secret',
  resave: false,
  saveUninitialized: false,
  cookie: { secure: false }  // For development,
set to false (use true in production with HTTPS)
}));

app.get('/', (req, res) => {
  if (req.session.views) {
    req.session.views++;
    res.send(`<h1>Views:
${req.session.views}</h1>`);
  } else {
    req.session.views = 1;
    res.send('<h1>Welcome    to    the    Node.js
App!</h1>');
  }
});

app.listen(3000, () => {
  console.log('Server          running          on
http://localhost:3000');
});
```

In this example:

343

- **express-session** is used to manage sessions.

- **Redis** is used as the session store via **connect-redis**.

- Each time the user visits the page, the **session views counter** is incremented and stored in Redis.

Real-World Example: Scaling a Social Media Application

Let's consider scaling a **social media application** built with Node.js. The app needs to handle user profiles, posts, comments, likes, and a large number of concurrent requests.

1. Initial Setup

The application architecture could include the following microservices:

- **User Service**: Manages user profiles and authentication.
- **Post Service**: Handles posts, likes, and comments.
- **Notification Service**: Manages real-time notifications for likes and comments.

2. Horizontal Scaling with Multiple Instances

1. **Docker Containers**: Use Docker to containerize each microservice and deploy them on multiple servers.

2. **Load Balancer**: Use an **NGINX** or **HAProxy** load balancer to distribute traffic across multiple instances of each service.

```
nginx

http {
    upstream user_service {
        server user-service-instance-1:3001;
        server user-service-instance-2:3001;
    }

    server {
        listen 80;

        location /users {
            proxy_pass http://user_service;
        }
    }
}
```

3. Redis for Caching and Session Management

Use **Redis** to manage sessions and cache frequently requested data, like user profiles and posts. This reduces database load and improves performance.

For example, you can cache user profiles in Redis to avoid querying the database on every request.

```javascript
const getUserProfile = async (userId) => {
  const         cachedProfile      =        await
redis.get(`user:${userId}`);
  if (cachedProfile) {
    return JSON.parse(cachedProfile);  // Return
cached data
  }

  // If not cached, fetch from the database
  const         userProfile        =        await
fetchUserFromDB(userId);

  // Cache the result for 1 hour
  redis.setex(`user:${userId}`,                3600,
JSON.stringify(userProfile));

  return userProfile;
};
```

4. Clustering the Application

For horizontal scaling, set up Node.js **clustering** to run multiple instances of each service across different servers or CPU cores.

```javascript
const cluster = require('cluster');
const numCPUs = require('os').cpus().length;
```

```
if (cluster.isMaster) {
  for (let i = 0; i < numCPUs; i++) {
    cluster.fork();
  }

  cluster.on('exit', (worker) => {
    console.log(`Worker    ${worker.process.pid}
died`);
  });
} else {
  require('./app');  // Your application code
}
```

Conclusion

In this chapter, we learned how to **scale Node.js applications** by implementing techniques such as **clustering**, **load balancing**, and **horizontal/vertical scaling**. We also explored **Redis** for **session management** and **caching** to enhance performance and scalability.

By adopting these strategies, you can build Node.js applications that are capable of handling high traffic and scaling effectively as the user base grows.

In the next chapter, we will focus on **performance tuning** and **optimization** techniques to further enhance your Node.js applications.

CHAPTER 27

FUTURE OF NODE.JS AND MODERN WEB DEVELOPMENT

Node.js has revolutionized the way we build server-side applications, and its ecosystem continues to evolve rapidly. As the demand for more scalable, efficient, and faster web applications grows, Node.js is well-positioned to adapt to emerging trends. In this final chapter, we will explore the **future of Node.js** in modern web development, looking at the **latest trends**, the rise of **serverless architecture**, and the impact of **edge computing**. We will also discuss what's next for Node.js and how you can prepare for it as a developer. Finally, we will wrap up with some **final thoughts** on how to build your next big project.

Trends in Node.js Development

Node.js has been growing rapidly over the past decade, and this trend is expected to continue. Here are some of the key trends shaping **Node.js development**:

1. Increased Use of Asynchronous Programming

As the need for high-performance applications rises, asynchronous programming will continue to be a significant focus in Node.js. With **async/await** becoming standard in JavaScript, **non-blocking I/O** in Node.js is more critical than ever. As applications become more real-time and data-intensive, Node.js's event-driven, non-blocking model allows developers to build scalable systems without worrying about blocking code.

2. Microservices and Modularization

The adoption of **microservices** and **modular architectures** is increasing. Developers are breaking down monolithic applications into smaller, independent services that can scale individually. Node.js is particularly well-suited for building these types of systems because it is lightweight, fast, and has great support for APIs and asynchronous operations.

3. Full-Stack JavaScript Development

Node.js has become a core part of the **full-stack JavaScript** development ecosystem. With tools like **Express**, **React**, **Angular**, **Vue**, and **Next.js**, JavaScript developers can now write both the client and server-side code in the same language. This allows for more seamless communication between front-end and back-end teams and accelerates development cycles.

350

4. Stronger Focus on Developer Tools and Ecosystem

The **Node.js ecosystem** continues to grow with powerful developer tools and libraries. Tools like **NPM**, **Webpack**, **Babel**, and **TypeScript** are increasingly used to streamline development processes. Node.js's growing ecosystem of frameworks, testing tools, and monitoring solutions enables developers to focus more on building and less on managing the complexity of their projects.

5. Enhanced Security Features

As Node.js gains more traction in enterprise applications, there's a growing need for **security**. The Node.js community is responding to this with better security features, libraries, and practices. **Secure APIs**, **authentication mechanisms**, and **encryption protocols** are becoming more standard as Node.js applications handle sensitive user data.

Serverless Architecture with Node.js

Serverless architecture allows developers to build and run applications without managing servers. In a serverless model, infrastructure management is handled by cloud providers like **AWS**, **Azure**, or **Google Cloud**, and developers only focus on writing the application logic. Node.js fits very well with this model because of its lightweight, event-driven nature.

351

1. Benefits of Serverless Architecture:

- **Scalability**: Serverless platforms automatically scale with demand.
- **Cost Efficiency**: Pay only for the compute resources you use, rather than maintaining a fixed number of servers.
- **Focus on Code**: Developers don't have to worry about provisioning or managing servers, which accelerates the development process.

2. Node.js and Serverless Frameworks

Several frameworks and platforms facilitate serverless application development, such as:

- **AWS Lambda**: A serverless compute service that supports Node.js, allowing you to run code without provisioning or managing servers.
- **Serverless Framework**: A popular open-source framework that simplifies building and deploying serverless applications. It supports multiple cloud providers, including AWS, Google Cloud, and Azure.

Example of setting up an AWS Lambda function using Node.js:

```javascript
exports.handler = async (event) => {
```

```
const responseMessage = 'Hello from AWS Lambda
with Node.js!';

  return {
    statusCode: 200,
    body:          JSON.stringify({          message:
responseMessage }),
  };
};
```

This serverless architecture is great for applications that require **scalable**, **cost-effective**, and **easy-to-maintain** solutions.

The Rise of Edge Computing

Edge computing refers to processing data closer to the source of data generation rather than in a centralized data center. This trend is becoming more relevant as the **Internet of Things (IoT)** grows and as applications need to process data faster with minimal latency.

In **edge computing**, computations are done at the **edge** of the network (closer to the user), which helps reduce latency and improves the speed and responsiveness of applications.

1. Node.js in Edge Computing

Node.js is an excellent fit for edge computing due to its event-driven, non-blocking architecture. Many edge computing platforms use lightweight Node.js servers to process data at the edge and then sync it with the central cloud infrastructure.

- **Low Latency**: With its non-blocking, asynchronous nature, Node.js excels at handling requests quickly and efficiently, making it a perfect candidate for edge environments.
- **IoT Applications**: As Node.js is fast and scalable, it is ideal for building IoT applications that require processing large amounts of data at the edge.

2. Edge Computing Platforms

- **Cloudflare Workers**: A platform that allows developers to run JavaScript code on the edge, closer to the user.
- **AWS Lambda@Edge**: Extends AWS Lambda's serverless computing capabilities to the edge of Amazon's content delivery network (CDN).

With edge computing, Node.js applications can provide faster and more responsive services, particularly for real-time applications.

What's Next for Node.js in Web Development?

As Node.js continues to evolve, we can expect several important trends and updates in the coming years:

1. Improved Native Support for TypeScript

TypeScript is becoming increasingly popular in the JavaScript ecosystem, and Node.js is expected to continue enhancing its support for **TypeScript**. With TypeScript, developers can benefit from static type-checking and enhanced IDE support, which makes large-scale Node.js applications more manageable and less error-prone.

2. Enhanced Performance and Optimizations

Node.js is constantly improving its performance, with each new release introducing optimizations for better handling of concurrent requests, memory management, and overall speed. We can expect Node.js to continue evolving with features like **worker threads, faster HTTP handling,** and **improved garbage collection**.

3. Better Integration with Modern Web Technologies

Node.js will continue to integrate with modern web technologies such as **GraphQL, WebSockets,** and **real-time communication**. The **microservices architecture** will be the standard for building

355

distributed systems, and Node.js will remain a popular choice for managing microservices, thanks to its **asynchronous nature**.

4. Growing Ecosystem of Tools and Libraries

As the ecosystem around Node.js expands, we can expect new tools and libraries that make development faster, easier, and more efficient. Libraries that improve debugging, testing, and monitoring will continue to evolve, making Node.js even more developer-friendly.

Final Thoughts and Building Your Next Big Project

As Node.js continues to be a powerful and versatile tool for modern web development, it's crucial to stay on top of new trends and best practices to build **scalable**, **efficient**, and **maintainable** applications. Whether you're building a **REST API**, **GraphQL API**, a **real-time chat app**, or a **microservices architecture**, Node.js is capable of handling it all.

Building Your Next Big Project with Node.js:

1. **Start Small**: Begin by building a small project to learn the ropes of Node.js and the latest technologies like **GraphQL**, **serverless**, or **microservices**.

2. **Use Modern Tools**: Take advantage of **TypeScript**, **GraphQL**, and **Apollo Server** to build modern, scalable applications.

3. **Focus on Performance**: As your application grows, consider using **clustering**, **load balancing**, and **Redis** to improve performance and scalability.

4. **Stay Updated**: Node.js is continuously evolving, so stay updated with the latest releases, features, and best practices to keep your projects current and competitive.

By using **Node.js** in combination with modern technologies like **GraphQL**, **serverless**, and **edge computing**, you'll be well-positioned to build the next big thing in web development. Your ability to adapt to new trends and tools will be key in the fast-moving world of software development.

This concludes our book on **Node.js for Modern Web Development**. I hope it has provided you with the knowledge, insights, and tools you need to embark on your journey to becoming a Node.js expert. Build boldly, and keep pushing the boundaries of web development with Node.js!

www.ingramcontent.com/pod-product-compliance
Lightning Source LLC
LaVergne TN
LVHW051428050326
832903LV00030BD/2975

9 7 9 8 3 1 6 8 7 9 3 3 5